THREE IMPOSSIBLE PRC

"This is a story of the transforming power of culture. In our focus on strategy, we often overlook the reality that culture - deep relationships of mutual respect - drives everything. In my time at P&G, I regularly saw cultural realities trump everything - trust in the organization determined the fate of every CEO. This is what Jesus modeled - influence the lives of 12 people deeply and build a culture of trust and honor. Then watch these ordinary people bring the strategy to life among the crowds and eventually the world."

Denis Beausejour
Pastor and former Global VP of Marketing, Procter & Gamble

"Three Impossible Promises is a wonderful story that will touch your heart and inspire you to think differently about the workplace and the importance of organizational culture. It weaves the power of untold human potential, breakthrough business success, and timeless Christian values into a tapestry that only God could have created. It's a great read, and it sends you forward with simple, practical ways to start reaping the benefits right now."

Matthew Kelly
New York Times Bestselling author of *The Dream Manager*

"Three Impossible Promises is an excellent book containing evidence of how God sometimes intervenes in our everyday lives in order to fulfill His will on earth. This is a compelling read containing passion, dedication and team work and, it shows how team and corporate culture is critical for long term success. In particular, this true story shows how success and life flow when we follow the Makers Instructions!"

Gerard Long
Executive Director, Alpha USA

THREE
IMPOSSIBLE
PROMISES

THREE
IMPOSSIBLE
PROMISES

THE INSPIRING TRUE STORY OF OLYMPIC GOLD
AND HOW ORGANIZATIONAL CULTURE MEANS EVERYTHING

GERRY PREECE
LYNNE RUHL

buckdale
PUBLISHING

Published in the United States by Buckdale Publishing,
3158 Hawkslanding Drive, Cincinnati, Ohio, 45244.

ISBN: 978-0-9854427-1-2

CONTENTS

--- PART 4 ---
GOLD

--- PART 5 ---
LESSONS

*This book is dedicated to leaders –
especially to those leaders who know that leadership is
a profound responsibility, who are aware that true
leadership is a rare though desperately needed thing,
and who believe that leadership is indeed a special and
perhaps even sacred calling.*

PREFACE

What can a hard-nosed, real world business leader
possibly learn from a girls' gymnastics team
that competed more than a decade ago?

Do you think your business is tougher than little girls' gymnastics? I did.

I loved it when I first heard the story that's in this book, but my initial thought, my immediate *objection,* really was, "Yeah, but I live in the real world." I spent four years at West Point, five more in the Army, and twenty-plus at Procter & Gamble. Many of my clients today are blue collar manufacturing types, guys with roughneck employees and heavy equipment. They deal with fistfights and stolen inventory and unannounced OSHA inspections, with disgruntled employees and physical threats. Their competitors are trying to steal their customers and are lying and selling below cost to do it. This is the real business world and these people aren't seven year old girls.

I'll give you the same challenge I gave myself. Go visit a competitive gym. Don't watch gymnastics on TV; see it in person. Like hockey and NASCAR, television doesn't do justice to this sport. Get to a competitive gym. Watch girls hitting a vault table at breakneck speed and spinning through the air before landing. Watch their dismounts from the uneven bars, and be sure to check their elevation. Think about what has to happen for them to try the next new maneuver, the next technique or skill that they haven't yet tried. How much courage and determination do they need? How much drive? How much intensity? Talk to a few of them during the break; see if you can tell a bit about what they're made of. Test their mettle a bit. Go ahead.

Think it's all about God-given natural ability? Ask them how many hours they've already put in this week, and ask them what else they're involved with at school and at home. Ask them how many injuries they've had and how they happened. Ask them what they did after their "little accidents." Ask them what parts of their bodies they had to ice down last night just to get to sleep. Call me and I'll arrange for you to chat with Lynne Ruhl's daughter, Becky. You can ask her about the *thirty-two* broken bones she managed to earn during her decade of "little girls' gymnastics."

If you're really courageous, ask to sign a waiver and see if they'll let you use some equipment after the competitive girls have left the floor. Try a handspring on the floor. Just try it. Stand on the beam and walk to the center; it's not that hard. Think about doing a back summersault and landing perfectly on the floor. Think about pointing your toes while you're doing it, about keeping your knees and ankles together, about kicking up, not out. Think about getting maximum height and tucking tightly. Think about doing it better than anyone else in the world. Okay, what about just getting into the top five hundred? Congratulations – you just *imagined* doing something most of these kids do every day without blinking. For warm-ups. Ask them again about those broken bones…

Don't let those cute girls in leotards fool you. They're stone cold gladiators. Hard work is hard work. Courage is courage. Determination and persistence and a passionate commitment to excellence are no different in your workplace than in a competitive gym. Coaches and athletes are striving mightily to do things better today than they did yesterday, and better than they even thought possible. They're going after the competition with all they've got. Gyms are dangerous places; people get hurt.[1] Dreams get crushed. Failures overwhelm people. Competitive gymnastics isn't tiddlywinks, and it isn't a "little girls' sport." It's tough stuff. It's demanding. It's fiercely, relentlessly competitive. And it's every bit as tough as anything you'll ever face in the real world workplace.

As a reference for the reader,
a brief primer on women's competitive gymnastics
appears in the Appendix, page 167.

---

[1] Multiple sources, including the National Center for Catastrophic Injuries Research, list gymnastics as one of the most dangerous sports of all. In terms of catastrophic injuries, it ranks third, just behind ice hockey and football, and more dangerous than lacrosse, basketball, soccer, and wrestling. In terms of overall injuries, it's number five, more dangerous overall than hockey, soccer, wrestling, and basketball.

"Culture eats strategy for breakfast."

Peter Drucker

THREE IMPOSSIBLE PROMISES

INTRODUCTION

WHY THIS BOOK WAS WRITTEN

A few years ago I met a woman named Lynne Ruhl, a small business owner in Cincinnati. Several of my business associates and friends had been telling me for months that I just absolutely had to meet this lady. So I finally did. I was reluctant to spend my time on what I thought would be just another networking meeting, never imagining that I would later become directly involved in her business. I finally agreed to meet her one afternoon at a local coffee shop, where we met and sipped sodas and chatted. She was nice. At first, she seemed maternal and simple, gentle and plain spoken. I found her to be a likeable but generally average and fairly unremarkable person in almost every way.

Then I heard her story.

I listened as Lynne described her business, Perfect 10 Corporate Cultures, as she spelled out what she did and why. The *why* fascinated me. The *why*, as it turned out, was deeply and profoundly rooted in her experience as Culture Manager for Cincinnati Gymnastics Academy (CGA) in the 1980's and 1990's. The *why*, I came to believe, applies to all of us, to you and to me and to our business endeavors, and especially to those who lead others. This book is really Lynne's story. It is about *why* she does what she does. It is about what she learned at CGA.

I tell this story purely from Lynne's perspective. I have talked to CGA's gold medalists, to CGA students and CGA's world class coach, to CGA's top tier sports psychologist from that era, to past employees, staff members, parents, and athletes. But this story is not democratically told. It is told as Lynne's reality; it is told as she experienced it. It is not a biography. It is not a historical account of all that went on in that gym. It is Lynne's story; it is her truth. I tell it as truthfully as I can, having only changed the names of some gymnasiums and a few of the story's characters.

At its core, this is a story about beliefs. It's about what we at Perfect 10 Corporate Cultures believe and the reasons for those beliefs, though the reasons are less important. Reasons are always thin when it comes to beliefs. They are always murky and hollow and unconvincing. If the reasons were crystal clear and compelling, we wouldn't need beliefs because we would *know*. Beliefs are *beliefs* because they connect and blossom not so much in our minds but rather in our hearts. They are not something we calculate and arrive at, decide upon and conclude. Rather, they are something we discover was planted inside us when we were first formed. Beliefs are not gentle. They are thundering things thrust upon us, and they consume our very lives and drive us ever forward.

At Perfect 10 Corporate Cultures, this is what we *believe*:

We believe that people are more valuable than you can know, that when people understand their uniqueness and have a safe place to bring it out and use it, they excel. And we believe that most of us, as leaders, vastly underestimate the talent and potential in our midst. The hard thing isn't finding the right talent. The truly hard thing is bringing it to the surface and unleashing it.

We believe that the time has come when it's no longer okay to do business in a way that leaves people as collateral damage. We believe that workplace leaders are called to lead, especially in areas of culture, and that they are anointed for their unique roles. We believe that leaders have a special and sacred calling, that they are responsible and accountable for establishing cultures in which people are treated with respect, not because of what they deliver or how they perform, but simply because of their inherent human dignity. We believe leaders are called to create places of integrity, where trust lives because people do what they say they will do, where promises are kept, and where everyone participates in creating an accountable culture. We believe leaders are called to create places where people challenge and confront one another in healthy, constructive ways. We believe that the primary job of a leader is to create and manage culture. We believe *you* are that leader and that through the workplace culture you create, you literally have the power to change the world. That is what we believe.

This is also a story about what we know to be true. Unlike beliefs, knowledge is something we do indeed think through and rationally conclude. We *know* things because we, the jury, have sat in the courtroom of life and business, and we have studied all the evidence. We have arrived at rock solid conclusions backed by inescapable logic that overwhelms any degree of reasonable doubt. We *know* things because we see the proof.

At Perfect 10 Corporate Cultures, this is what we *know*:

We know that when leaders deliberately establish a cultural foundation of respect and trust, human performance soars. We know that when leaders do these things, they produce better performance, higher revenue and profits, and more satisfied customers. We know that when leaders fail at these things, it is most often because they lack the skill and know-how, not the desire. We also know that they don't need to always get the culture perfect. They can and do succeed despite their own human shortcomings, and even though the cultures they create may remain imperfect. We know that leaders who do these things also do something immeasurably more. Leaders who do these things make a profound difference in the lives of people. They enable a kind of human fulfillment in the workplace – and in the world beyond it – that has rarely been known, and they unleash the awesome power of human compassion and character that our world so badly needs. We know workplace leaders can do *both*. They can treat people the right way *and* have fantastic success in business and the workplace.

We know that this is not an act of careful balancing, not a way of keeping competing ideas in careful check. Rather, we know it is a long overdue marriage, a sort of blessed synergy, and its time has finally arrived.

> Healthy cultures and good business results are not competing ideas to be balanced and kept in check. Just the opposite: they are perfectly complimentary and synergistic, a long overdue marriage.

We know that culture matters more than strategy, because a poor culture cannot implement a great strategy; yet even a mediocre strategy executed by a great culture wins.

At Perfect 10 Corporate Cultures, we live for the day when organizational culture takes its rightful place in the workplace, fully embraced as the single greatest lever to achieving performance, profits and results. We live for the day when cultures of profound respect and human dignity will be commonplace. That's why we do what we do. That's what drives us. That's why I'm writing this book, and why I ask that you share this message with others.

Our founder served as Culture Manager for Cincinnati Gymnastics Academy, which went from humble and toxic beginnings to become a world renowned training facility for Olympic gold medalists. In the process, a global industry was transformed, and organizational culture took center stage in one of the most unlikely and remarkable success stories of our time. It is a story that will touch your heart and ignite your deeply held beliefs about people, workplace culture and performance. And it is a story that will provide evidence, courtroom proof, that when leadership gets the culture right, human performance soars beyond anything we can comprehend.

This is that story. We hope it will become *yours*.

PART ONE

UNQUALIFIED

CHAPTER 1

THE
PHONE CALL

The sound of the phone ringing came as it always does, jarring and out of the blue, yet familiar. But this time it would change everything. She wouldn't understand that until years later, of course, she had no inkling of its significance when she answered.

Even after she hung up, Lynne Ruhl counted this as just another phone conversation and a mild distraction. She could not have been more wrong.

When the phone rang, Lynne put down her Bible on the coffee table beside the overstuffed living room chair she had settled into. She reached over and hit the pause button on the cassette player, which had been gently filling the room with the haunting voice of Nancy Honeytree, singing from her Maranatha Marathon album on the Myrrh Records label. It was 1983, and Honeytree was making it big in Christian music. It took Lynne a moment and some conscious effort to come out of her deep immersion in study.

"Hello?"

"Mrs. Ruhl?"

"Yes."

"Hi, Lynne, this is Dave Jones, at the gym. I'm calling about your daughter, Becky."

"Oh, my gosh. Hi Dave. Is everything okay?"

"Well, yes, Becky's fine. Nothing to be concerned about. Actually just the opposite," said Dave.

"Oh? So tell me what's going on."

Dave said, "Lynne, I have been coaching Becky for a few months now, and she's a real delight to work with. She's a great little kid. You know, she really seems to love gymnastics, and she has a real aptitude for it. She's got lots of enthusiasm. It's so surprising to see that in a seven year old. Frankly, she's head and shoulders better than all the other girls I coach in her neighborhood group; there's just no comparison."

Lynne felt the pride that all parents do when they hear that their child is excelling at something.

"Oh, that's so good to hear, Dave. I so appreciate all you do with her," Lynne said with genuine sincerity.

"Today I tried something, just as a sort of experiment," Dave said, his voice ticked up a notch in energy and enthusiasm. "The older girls, the eight and nine year olds, were having bit of an informal competition, just among themselves. Well, I decided to let Becky work with them just for this one session, and Lynne, it seemed to me she performed better than all of them."

Lynne was blushing now, proud but a bit uncomfortable with such a glowing report. Every parent wants their kid to do well. But parents also feel uncomfortable when children do so well that they become "different." Lynne didn't know how to respond, nor did she yet know what Dave wanted – had he called simply to report on Becky's progress? She just listened.

Dave continued, "Well, it's pretty unusual to see that kind of talent in a girl so young. I mean, she's pretty darned good and frankly I'd like to move her up from the neighborhood group to the competitive program. The hitch is that we don't have a competitive program for her age group right now, but I'd like to move her up anyway. I know she's only seven but I can put her up with the eight and nine year olds and I really think she'll do fine despite the age difference."

"Uh huh…" Lynne was listening, taking it all in, but in her mind she wasn't sure she wanted this for Becky. This thought triggered the next, raised her awareness that she wasn't even sure what moving Becky into competitive gymnastics really entailed. Mostly she wanted to slow things down and take some time to think it through. She sensed that Dave was about to ask her permission to move Becky into the competitive program, and Lynne wasn't ready to give an answer.

After a long moment Lynne said, "Gee, I'm going to have to digest this, Dave. I knew she has been having fun there and that she loves gymnastics, but I honestly didn't know she was doing *that* well."

Lynne thought back on how all this had started and smiled to herself. Her mother, Lynne's mother, wanted to spend time with Becky, to have something that was just for the two of them, a way to bond granddaughter to grandmother and create some memories together. "Would you rather do dance or gymnastics?" Grandma had asked little Becky, back when she was only three years old, as if there were no other choices to be considered by a grandmother and granddaughter who wanted to spend time together. "Gymnastics!" Becky had replied, without hesitation, Lord knows why. But she absolutely loved her gymnastics sessions and loved her time with Grandma. Lynne didn't want to disrupt that, and wondered to herself if "competitive gymnastics" would mean changing all that.

Lynne asked, "Competitive gymnastics? I have no idea what that is. What would it mean for us, Dave?"

Dave answered, "Well, for starters, instead of one hour each week, it will mean eleven hours. With that group we do two hours most days and – "

"Eleven hours a week? Are you serious? She's only seven!"

"Afraid, so, Lynne," Dave said. "But the good news is that she'll be learning a lot more and will be in with kids that are really good, and all that will help her grow into a better gymnast. I know she's good enough to do it, and I think she'll love it. And in the worst case, if it ends up not being for her, you can always drop Becky back into the neighborhood program."

Lynne considered this for a long moment.

Dave said, "I know she'll love it, Lynne. And I'd hate to see a kid with her kind of talent not have it developed. Even if she fizzles out, it seems to me you still have to give a kid with her potential a shot."

"Wow," Lynne replied. "Okay, okay. You've thrown a lot at me, Dave. I really appreciate your calling me and I'll think about this, and I'll talk it over with Roger when he gets home from work tonight. We'll let you know whatever we decide."

They said their goodbyes, and Lynne hung up the phone and returned to where she had been studying the Bible. But it was impossible to recapture her trance-like concentration from earlier, and after some minutes of trying, she finally took the portable cassette player into the kitchen, pushed the 'play' button, and set about the business of preparing dinner.

Still invisible to her, the grand, cosmic gears of transformation had engaged and had slowly begun to turn. Their work would take some time, but the eventual results would be undeniable, and Lynne Ruhl's world would never be the same.

It seems the greatest, most pivotal moments of our lives always come at us like this, disguised as common, unremarkable events, like everyday visitors. They don't arrive loudly or with fanfare, not in fancy suits or flashy neckties, not in evening gowns nor in fashionable, sequined styles. They tap gently on our door and we, preoccupied with the relentless though mundane concerns of our lives, greet the things as the humdrum visitors they appear to be, dressed in jeans and tee shirts as they are.

How many of them have we dismissed, unaware of their significance, oblivious to their fantastic power and promise, which we cannot see until after we have embraced them, until after they have changed the course of our lives and years have passed?

Is there a visitor at your door, right now, that might later prove to be life changing?

CHAPTER 2

DINNER

Lynne loved hosting these kinds of gatherings. They were informal and fun, and staying connected with family was something she truly treasured. Margaret (Lynne's mother, Becky's grandmother) would be home with Becky soon, and Lynne's twenty-six year old younger brother, Brad, would arrive around six o'clock, just in time for dinner. Becky also loved these get-togethers, and she especially looked forward to seeing Uncle Brad, her "all-time most favorite uncle in the whole wide world," as he had taught her to say when she was just learning to string words together, and which she always said with authentic joy and conviction.

Lynne's husband, Roger, had called to say he'd be home late – again. Lynne had gotten used to Roger's working late at his job in marketing for the Cincinnati Reds. Lynne and Roger met while she was also part of the Reds organization, helping to manage their radio and gift shop operations. The era of the Big Red Machine had just passed, and the Reds organization was flailing around a bit, struggling to find a way to somehow keep the magic going. They had picked up the aging Tom Seaver and had been experimenting with Johnny Bench at third base. The city knew its baseball, and fans found the moves puzzling at best. The dynasty was in decline, and the Reds management knew it. Marketing to the rescue – and that meant endless hours for Roger, who truth be told, loved it. They could talk about the competitive gymnastics thing on the weekend.

Lynne put the lasagna in the oven and the delightful scents of sweet basil, oregano, and roasted garlic soon wafted their way through her kitchen. She put the tea kettle on the stove, and before it boiled into its whistle, Margaret arrived with Becky, still in her leotard and still bursting with energy.

"Is Uncle Brad here, Mom?"

"Not yet, honey, but he'll be here soon. He called from the airport, said he's already done with his flying and is heading toward his car. Said he can't wait to see you." Brad was a pilot and flew small commercial cargo jets for a living. Unlike Roger's job, Brad's profession consumed him in chunks, keeping him out of town and busy for a few days in a row, and then returned him home for a few uninterrupted days of recuperation and family time. Satisfied that her all-time favorite uncle in the whole wide world would arrive soon, Becky radiated delight and bounced up the stairs toward her room and a change of clothes.

"Hi, Mom. How'd it go today?" Lynne asked her mother, not sure if Margaret was aware of what Dave had said to her about Becky.

"Hello, Lynne." Margaret said to her daughter. "Becky and I had another wonderful day. That little girl *loves* her gymnastics and she just bubbles about it all the way there, all through her sessions, and all the way home." Then she leaned in toward Lynne and added in a conspiratorial tone, "That kid doesn't shut up the entire time!" Margaret brightened with an easy smile and winked at Lynne. She cherished these sessions with her granddaughter, these little interludes in her life when it was just the two of them. The seven year old and the fifty-something grandma built a familiar trust, shared innocent secrets, and relished the carefree delight of play – and sometimes the joy of a McDonald's ice cream afterward. Apparently Margaret did not know about Dave's phone call.

Lynne laughed. She knew Becky's boundless energy could be a lot for any adult, especially for someone who might be looking to slow down some. "She'll keep you young, won't she," Lynne said, chuckling.

Margaret sat heavily into a kitchen chair and sighed, glad to have had the time with her special little girl and relieved that she could finally rest and catch her breath. Just as she sat down the boiling teapot whistled that it was ready, and Lynne poured them both a cup.

Lynne sat down and stole a long glance at her mother from across the kitchen table, through the lifting mist that arose like incense from the hot cups of tea that had just been poured.

"I love you, Mom," came out of Lynne before she even knew she was saying it. "Thanks for all you do with Becky. She loves her time with you."

Margaret smiled in acknowledgement. "So how are you, Lynne? Tell me about the latest with your Bible Study."

"Oh, Mom, thanks for asking. I know you think I go overboard on this, but I just feel like I can't get enough." Lynne had recently embraced Christianity, after years of searching. Something deeply spiritual in her had hungered for more, for an answer to that 'isn't there more to life?' question, and she spent years seeking out something that connected with her soul. She finally found it at a small church in Cincinnati's College Hill community. Since her conversion and her decision to commit herself to following the teachings of Christ, she had been studying and researching and reading everything she could find on the topic. Lynne felt the incredible excitement of faith, of pure conviction that went beyond reason, and had urgently set about the business of learning all she could as fast as she could. "I feel like I have this new best friend, Mom. A new best friend named Jesus – but I still feel like I know so very little about Him. I want to know everything there is to know. Even with that, I know for sure He's the most important thing in my life, the most important thing ever. I feel like I just won't be denied any more and I'm trying to learn all I can about Him. I want it all, Mom. I'm asking Him to share it *all* with me."

Just then there was a light tap on the front door, and then it opened. Brad came through, grinning big. "Hiya, Lynne. Hi Mom. Wow, it smells great in here!"

"Hi Brad," the two women said in unison, tea steam still gently rising between them. They popped up and hugged the son and brother they loved and admired so much. Brad was that rare young man who always did the right thing, treated others with kindness, and carried a fun-loving joy that others found contagious.

"Becky can't wait to see you," Lynne reported. "She's upstairs getting changed and ought to be down any minute."

Brad beamed, went to the bottom of the stairs and yelled up, "Hey Squirt, what are you doing up there? Come on down!" The adults all heard Becky's shriek of delight from upstairs, and in a flash the seven year old reached the bottom of the stairs.

"Uncle Brad – my all-time most favorite uncle in the whole wide world!" Becky gave Brad a hug and ushered him into the kitchen. As they walked, Brad tapped Becky on the far shoulder, the one opposite him, and the seven year old turned and looked over her shoulder to see who it was. She fell for the gag before she recognized it was a ruse, and it was obvious she loved it. A few steps more and he flipped at her hair and flicked a finger at her ear, with Becky giggling and poking him back each time. The best uncle in the whole wide world....

The four of them shared a wonderful dinner together. It wasn't particularly significant nor did it mark any special milestone in their family's history. It was indeed truly wonderful, but only in the sense that four people who loved one another deeply shared a meal and

companionship. The salad, the lasagna, the rolls were fine. The experience of friendship, of trust and belonging, were quietly spectacular.

When dinner ended they eventually said their goodbyes and goodnights, and pledged to get together again soon. They had no way of knowing it would never happen again.

Becky with her Uncle Brad

CHAPTER 3

SEARCHING FOR A GYM

The conversation with Roger went smoothly. They talked to Becky first, and it was clear she wanted to do it; she was thrilled with the idea. Lynne and Roger agreed that it seemed like the best thing for Becky was to put her into a competitive gymnastics program. They also agreed they should be deliberate about choosing the right gym. They didn't take for granted that Becky should simply stay at GymPerfect and just move up to the competitive program there. Lynne had called Becky's old pre-school gymnastics teacher, Mary Lee Tracy for advice, and Mary Lee suggested Lynne look carefully at the various competitive programs in the city before making her choice. When three year old Becky first started gymnastics, then nineteen year old Mary Lee was her coach, at least to the extent one can say that three year olds have "coaches." Regardless, Mary Lee was great with the kids, and Lynne could see that Mary Lee was the key reason why Becky fell in love with the sport.

In addition to Mary Lee's advice, which Lynne weighed heavily, Lynne herself wanted to do her own research before choosing the right competitive gym. If she were going to arrange for somebody to coach her daughter for eleven hours each week, Lynne wanted to know who the person was, how they behaved, and what the place was like. She wanted to see how they handled the competitive gymnastics kids during practices and in meets. She wasn't about to let anyone have that much influence over her seven year old daughter without first vetting the people and place pretty thoroughly.

There was a general buzz about women's gymnastics at the time. Nadia Comaneci had become wildly popular as a result of her first-ever, perfect 10.0 performance in the 1976 Olympics, and *Nadia's Theme* could be heard in gymnasiums everywhere. Just a few months later, Mary Lou Retton would win America's heart by becoming the first American woman in history to win the Olympic All-Around gold. The sport of women's gymnastics was becoming wildly popular in America. Little girls all across Cincinnati, and all across the country for that matter, wanted to try their skill at the sport and see if they might be able to unite themselves with their Olympic heroes.

GymOhio would be first, Lynne decided. It was nearby, and she heard it was one of the best known competitive gyms in the city. Lynne was surprised at how many cars were in the parking lot for GymOhio, and she took note of the parents and youngsters of all ages who were coming and going in the busy parking lot. There seemed to be a quick-paced bustle to the place and a general tone of seriousness evident on many of the faces. These were not the faces she had seen on Becky and her friends when they returned from workouts with Dave, she thought to herself as she walked toward the gym's door.

Inside there was activity everywhere. Girls were running from left to right in front of Lynne and leaping into summersaults. Boys were working on pommel horses. Older girls were whirling around on uneven bars. Older boys were swinging from suspended rings and were leaping to lofty heights on trampolines. The blur of activity was dizzying at first. The youngest girls appeared to be only three, like Becky was when she first started, and they were cocooned in a thickly padded, walled off section. They seemed to be playing some kind of follow the leader game, jumping over small obstructions and tumbling easily at designated spots, marked by brightly colored, rolled up mats.

On the whole, Lynne found it chaotic and a bit overwhelming. Maybe I'll get used to it; maybe I'm just so new at all this, she thought to herself, amid the flurry of motion and popcorn popping of floor routines and vaulting. After ten minutes of trying in vain to decipher exactly what was going on, she headed to the folding chairs that were positioned behind a glass viewing wall and settled into the first empty seat. The lady next to her made eye contact and nodded, but there was no smile, no warmth in the acknowledgement. She seemed businesslike and aloof.

A young boy who appeared to be about two years old - Lynne guessed it was the lady's son - was standing in front of another folding chair and appeared to have intentionally pushed a few Crayons and a coloring book off the seat and watched them fall to the floor.

"Jeremy, pick that up this instant or I'll swat your backside! I'm not going to tell you again." The lady scolded her youngest child while never breaking her stare toward the gymnastics floor on the other side of the glass.

"Kids and Crayons," Lynne said with a smile toward the lady sitting beside her. This caused the woman to turn toward Lynne and smile a bit, but she seemed intent on watching what was happening on the gym floor.

"I take it you've got a son or daughter out there," said Lynne, trying to strike up some rapport. "I'm just visiting, trying to get a handle on competitive gymnastics for my seven year old daughter. Would you recommend this place?"

The lady turned fully toward Lynne and took a long pause before replying. "No. I definitely would not recommend this place. *Lots* of room for improvement. Plus they're full up on seven year olds already and the coaching is less than stellar. Jennifer would be at the next level already if they'd give her some attention and took note of her poise. It's pretty obvious she's better than kids at the next level; they just have their favorites, you know." The lady said all this flatly, without expression, and with more than a hint of frustration in her voice. She turned back to the activity on the floor and resumed her careful, attentive watching. The unspoken message to Lynne was that the lady was not interested in any extended conversation, and Lynne picked up the signal right away.

"Thanks for sharing that," said Lynne, who decided not to pursue things further. A few minutes later Lynne stood and mingled with a few other onlookers. She struck up similar conversations and got similar replies, though not quite as blunt as the first. The short exchanges all seemed a bit impersonal and ranged from cool indifference to polite disinterest. Not the warmest crowd she'd ever encountered, Lynne thought to herself. She headed toward the stairs and another viewing position.

From the second floor balcony, Lynne got a more comprehensive view of the place and soon was able to distinguish the more skilled and competitive groups from the less competitive ones. Young athletes were clustered in bunches, and Lynne could tell by the coaching, or the lack of it in many cases, where supervisory attention was being directed. She surveyed the floor and found what she guessed were girls of about age seven, who appeared to be in a competitive group. The more she studied the groups, the more obvious it became. The non-competitive kids were laughing and playfully flopping over foam barriers, while the competitive ones sprinted full out and attacked equipment with an entirely different level of intensity. There was no laughing, no joviality in the competitive group. It finally occurred to Lynne that they even dressed differently, and she wondered how it took her so long to notice something that was now so obvious. The neighborhood girls wore cute, loose fitting pink and grey outfits with stitched teddy bears on their sweatshirts and bright ribbons in their hair. The competitive girls wore form-fitting, skin-tight leotards. Their hair was pulled back and pinned into neat, tightly packed, rigid buns. Nearly all the coaching attention was directed towards a few competitive girls. The teenager that appeared to be in charge of the non-competitive kids went about her tasks casually, with a more lackadaisical posture. She seemed to be more concerned with her nearby peers than she was with her group of kids.

The competitive coaches, however, were anything but casual.

They glared at and stalked the competitive athletes as they practiced their routines. They either said nothing or shouted their disappointment in harsh, angry tones. "What's *wrong* with you, Carolyn? How many times do I have to tell you to tuck! Why am I wasting my time with you?" The girls seemed to handle it surprisingly well, at least on the surface, but Lynne watched several of them melt down when they came off the floor and approached their parents. Some of the parents seemed sympathetic to their wounded children, but one nearby parent piled on even harder. "I'm expecting you to win on Saturday, Carrie, and your performance today makes me wonder if you even belong on the floor."

Lynne didn't like what she was witnessing. She turned to the adults who like her, were watching the floor, and looked for a parent who might be inclined to share some perspective. She settled on a plain looking mom with mousy hair, wearing comfortable warm ups and smiling at her new baby, which she held in her arms. Her demeanor seemed much less intense and she looked easily approachable.

"Hi," Lynne said, as she made an effort to look sunny. "Do you mind if I sit here? Just couldn't help but notice your baby and you know we're all attracted to babies."

"Sure, have a seat," the pleasant woman replied.

After introductions and some small talk, Lynne eased her way around to the same question she had posed to the first woman. Was she happy with how her daughter was treated there; was she well coached; and most importantly, would the lady recommend this place for Becky?

"Oh, this place? It's great," the woman told her. "My daughter really seems to enjoy it and has made some good friends here. And they're good with the kids; they keep them busy and active." The lady brushed noses with her baby and unabashedly gushed some baby talk before turning back to Lynne. "It's a good place, and I'd recommend it to anyone. We're going to come here for you too, aren't we?" she chirped merrily to her infant.

Lynne asked, "Why have so many other people said the opposite to me? Why do you seem so happy and yet so many of them don't? Others said there were already too many kids in Becky's age group here, and they said the coaching was lousy. I wonder what the difference is."

"Oh," the lady responded with new clarity. "I'll bet you were talking to parents of the competitive kids, weren't you?"

"Yes, I was. Isn't your daughter in the competitive program?"

"Oh, no, not Lisa. Lisa's in the neighborhood group. That competitive program, that's another thing altogether."

"How so?"

"Well they're competitive – all the way, for starters. They're *all* competitive. I don't mean just the girls. I mean the darned parents are competitive. I'll bet they told you not to come here just because they don't want their precious ones to have to compete against yet one more girl. And coaches? The coaches are fine. Some of them even got recognized at the state level last year. It's just that you were talking to parents downstairs who wanted their girls to succeed, even at the expense of your daughter's growth."

Lynne was puzzled. "But don't the competitive girls here compete against the competitive girls from *other* gyms, not against the girls in this gym?"

"Yeah. *After* they make the team here. And some of them would rather be number one on this team, which is pretty mediocre, than number five on a better team."

And so went Lynne Ruhl's initial baptism into the world of competitive gymnastics. She listened carefully as the lady provided more insight and guidance, and Lynne did not feel very good about all she was hearing. She would keep an open mind, she decided, and would definitely visit other gyms in hopes that she'd find a better place for Becky.

CHAPTER 4

SEARCHING AGAIN

A few days later, Lynne drove to Pinnacle Gymnastics in the morning and then to Century One Gymnastics in the afternoon. The next day she visited GymPerfect and studied the competitive program Dave was recommending for Becky. Lynne saw more of the same: protective, guarded parents and intense young athletes. She saw competitive coaches yelling at kids and belittling them. Were they all like this? She visited Elite Petites the following Monday and then on Thursday she went to Cinci Gold. They were all disappointing. Finally there was just one gym left, and on Saturday morning Lynne walked through the front door of Losantiville Gymnastics, regarded by some as the best of the bunch. Immediately she felt the difference.

Losantiville appeared to be a more lighthearted place, more fun and less overtly intense. The kids seemed happy and there was a joyous buzz coming from the swarm of young girls on the floor. She watched the coaches, who all wore dark shirts with the Losantiville logo, and noted that they worked at being enthusiastic and encouraging. At the other gyms coaches dressed more or less randomly, and few, if any, could be called enthusiastic. Lynne considered the possibility that perhaps she'd finally found just the place for Becky.

"This place looks great," Lynne confided to the couple standing next to her, an older gentleman who Lynne imagined might be the grandfather of one of the girls on the floor. He smiled and agreed. Lynne went on. "I've been driving all around town trying to find the right gym for my daughter, who wants to do competitive gymnastics. Some of what I've seen hasn't been very good."

"Competitive?" the man asked. "Oh, these are just the neighborhood kids," the man told her. "Competitive kids are back there," and he nodded toward a red-walled hallway that led away from the large room they were in and disappeared around a corner.

Lynne slowly made her way toward the red corridor, a bit deflated from learning that the encouraging scene she had been watching was not the right group, but hoping that she'd nevertheless find a positive scene as she rounded the next corner.

* * * * * * *

The tall, mustached coach glowered at the young girl, who was wearing a navy leotard and appeared to be a few inches shorter than the other girls. The girl stood at rigid attention while the coach simply stared at her with an expression of condescending disgust. Lynne had been watching her for a few minutes and could easily see that the girl was one of the best athletes in the building. She had been practicing a dismount from the balance beam in which she dismounted from the middle of the beam by doing a back flip to the side of the beam, landing on the floor. The athlete, summoned by her coach, stood perfectly still and looked straight ahead, eyes empty and plain, not making eye contact with her coach. The tension was obvious.

He slammed the clipboard he had been carrying onto the floor, and this seemed to be some sort of unspoken signal to the entire gym of what was to come. Others promptly floated back and away, like grains of pepper on water's surface when a droplet of dish soap is placed in the center. All eyes had turned toward the two of them.

"The free leg swings UP, not out, Kelli! I don't know what it's going to take to get you to do it! You land okay, but you are going to lose points. I've had it with you! Are you listening? Do you *ever* listen? Swing the damn leg up! Up! Up!" She stared straight ahead and seemed to shrink before him, his tantrum and aggressive, forward-leaning posture making him appear even larger. Without touching her, he physically overwhelmed the little girl. "Now get up on that dammed beam and do it right!" Lynne's heart sank for the little girl as she watched the scene unfold.

With all the others watching, the young athlete propelled herself evenly and with minimum motion, like a machine, an automaton, toward the end of the beam and mounted, then collected herself and walked to the center. She paused for a long moment, concentrated, and raised both arms straight over her head. The gym was eerily silent and all other activity had slowed to a stop. On the beam, the girl leaned left and squatted a bit, swung her arms forcefully and executed a side back gainer dismount, as one of the nearby parents called it. Lynne couldn't tell if the girl had done what the coach wanted or not – did she swing her free leg upward enough, or was she still swinging it too far outward?

The coach carefully watched her dismount, scrutinized it closely with his eyes and his linebacker stance, fully attuned and ready to pounce. He held his pose for an exaggerated moment after her feet hit the floor mat, waited for her to fully finish her landing and turn toward him, obviously anxious for her coach's coming judgment. When she faced him, he made a dramatic show of pivoting and turning his back to her. His arms and shoulders slumped in disappointment. He rose up loosely from his pounce-ready crouch and dropped his head toward the floor in mock surrender. He slowly brought his fists to his hips and shook his head slowly from side to side. The student, the little girl, remained facing him, motionless and still at rigid attention.

In the silence of the cavernous room, the coach, who remained with his back to the little girl, belted out three long, sharp blows on the whistle that hung from his neck. The whistles instantly filled the emptiness, and sparked activity everywhere. Young, competitive gymnasts rushed forward from the edges of the room and flowed themselves into a large circle around the athlete who had apparently once again failed to properly swing her leg upward. Then a sprinting surge of new bodies appeared from the red hallway and poured themselves past the competitive athletes, toward the lone offender, who stood motionless and silent, her eyes on the floor. The newly arrived brigade of neighborhood gymnasts, casual students of the sport, formed an inner circle, inside the circle of competitive athletes, all surrounding the one lone girl in the middle. Still, utter silence.

"Kelli..." the coach finally bellowed to the whole congregation, still keeping his back to the girl in the middle. "Kelli won't do what I told her to do!" His damning judgment and condemnation was loud and plain, a formal proclamation of her guilt. He stood in their midst in complete control, a general amongst his troops before battle. "Kelli," he barked, "refuses to listen to me." Nobody moved.

His naming the girl, albeit in condemnation, finally humanized her for Lynne. When the coach used Kelli's name, it caused Lynne to look past the athlete and aspiring disciple and see the scared, insecure child. Lynne's heart broke for little Kelli, the eleven year old girl who was alone, afraid and overwhelmed.

The coach moved away from Kelli, never looking back at her. "What do we do to gymnasts who won't listen to their coach?" It was as if Kelli's public sentencing had been announced to the masses. Instantly, nearly one hundred girls in leotards and sweat suits whirled in unison and turned their back on Kelli. There was no sound but the swoosh of one hundred girls pivoting at once. "And, what do we think about her?"

With that prompt, all the girls began yelling at Kelli, ridiculing her and calling her names, while the coach strolled effortlessly, fully in control of the brutal affair. "Kelli is terrible!" came from some anonymous peer. "Do what your coach tells you, dummy!" from another. Girls spun to face Kelli as they screamed their accusations, then when finished, they spun back again so their back was to her while they thought up their next insult. It was vicious.

"You'll never learn!"

"Kelli is a fatty!"

"Get out of our gym!"

"What's wrong with you!?"

"Your dumb leotard looks stupid – just like you!"

"Cry baby Kelli! Cry! Cry!"

"Kelli, fatty, stupid, dumb Kelli!"

For twenty seconds this went on, unabated. Children screamed insults and barked out their disapproval, while the general strode through the ranks, nodding approvals at the attackers. And the girl in the middle stood and took it, eyes down, motionless and apparently forbidden to show any response or emotion. Lynne realized there must be an unwritten code – that to break down and cry in response to this punishment would be the worst thing of all. To cave in, to collapse in humiliation would be to fail altogether and probably meant outright dismissal from the gym. Kelli had to stand there. Kelli had to listen. Kelli had to take it. Kelli was forbidden to cry, to speak, to respond.

Lynne finally had to look away, and when she did, she became aware that her own hands were shaking, that her entire body was trembling in helpless anger. Overwhelmed, Lynne spun and walked crisply out of the gym, stupefied by the outrageous and hideous scene she had just witnessed. She ached for little Kelli and choked in her own guilt – I should have done something! Yet she had no idea what she could have said or done that would have made things better. She fumbled for keys, still shaking in anger, and sat in her car for several seconds before hot angry tears came pouring out. Eventually, she took a few deep breaths and calmed down enough to find the ignition and sufficiently collected her wits so she could drive.

She finally pointed her car toward home and eased into the lane of traffic, still in a state of stunned disbelief. The steady, regular drone of traffic seemed to calm her and gradually eased her back toward reality. "I will never, ever, allow that to happen to Becky, so help me God..." Lynne said out loud to nobody but herself and her car. The words came from some place deep and they came unsummoned, came of their own will. "Never!"

At the highest levels, elite women gymnasts spend in the neighborhood of twenty-four hours per week training. Many of them live away from their families in order to train at the best gyms. They often delay their schooling, including college, to compete. They give up normal teenage rites of passage, like vacations, trips to the pool with friends, proms, homecoming, and club activities. It costs them – financially, emotionally, and physically. Most are in their mid-teens. Their competitive fires burn hot.

CHAPTER 5

UNLIKELY DECISION

She had rehearsed the whole conversation in her mind before they sat down. She had practiced her arguments and honed and polished how she'd present the evidence when Roger resisted. She knew exactly how she'd open the discussion, as it would direct the rest of the conversation and would help drive the conclusion she wanted, which was to keep Becky in neighborhood gymnastics with Dave Jones.

"Roger," Lynne said, "do you remember when I told you about Dave Jones calling from the gym, and suggesting we put Becky in a competitive program?"

"Sure. Did you get a chance to check out the gyms like you planned to do?"

"I did… what I saw was pretty bad. The bottom line is that I wouldn't feel comfortable with putting Becky in any of the programs I saw."

"Oh, that's disappointing."

"Roger," Lynne said with complete confidence, "if Becky is ever going to do competitive gymnastics, we're going to have to buy a gym." Lynne thought that would be the end of it, that it would finally put the whole competitive gymnastics thing to rest once and for all. What she hadn't counted on was that Roger had been wrestling for weeks with Lynne's increasing religiosity, and part of him had been searching in vain for something to occupy her time, to consume her, to give her some more practical yet still noble thing to do. That and the fact that his good work at the Reds was earning him a bonus that he knew was coming. But he had not yet shared this news with Lynne. They'd soon be flush with some extra cash, and it needed a place to land.

"Okay." Roger's abrupt, one word reply came out of his mouth before he was aware of it, but he didn't regret it. It was as if something deep in him immediately saw the rightness of this unlikely plan before his conscious self could even consider the pros and cons. Not that these thoughts were far behind; it didn't take long for anyone to see how foolish it would be to just go out and buy a gym.

They stared at each other for a moment, both blinking in disbelief. Neither one of them expected this; they both knew how ridiculous this was. Yet both also had a gut instinct that it was absolutely the perfect thing to do. Surprisingly, they didn't discuss it further. Not a word. They both instinctively knew that any rational assessment of the decision would only serve to illuminate the hundreds of reasons why it made no sense. For one, Roger had zero capacity to engage on something like this, so it would have to be completely Lynne's endeavor. They had absolutely no experience with running anything like a gym – didn't even know where to start, for another. Buying any business, especially a business in a field they knew nothing about, would be fraught with costly, painful surprises for any newcomer. What were the legal considerations? Cash flow? Hiring and firing laws? How do you set prices? What about certifications? The dizzying list went on and on, but strangely, meant almost nothing in that moment.

Yet they both recognized that something stirred them in a deeper way. Call it gut instinct or intuition. Call it a guardian angel or God's whisperings. Call it subconscious or that quiet voice inside. Whatever it was, it spoke to Lynne and Roger Ruhl and told them that it was okay – more than okay, really. It seemed to say that they *should* do this, that it was the *right* thing to do. It made no sense whatsoever. But they would do it. And that voice, that instinct was so clear that they never questioned it. They said yes, and their lives would never be the same.

They met with a lawyer the following week and it was agreed that a blind letter would go out from the lawyer's office. "My unnamed client is interested in buying your gymnasium," it started. It was a complete long shot. But sure enough, three weeks later, negotiations began in earnest with John Thomas, then the owner of Cincinnati Gymnastics Academy.

That's when reality struck Lynne. Who's going to run the place? How do you actually teach and coach gymnastics? Where do you even learn about gymnastics? And do we really want to invest our hard earned savings in this crazy venture? Lynne was beginning to have doubts. The more she thought, the more doubts crept in. Lynne turned to prayer, as she often had. The irony would be lost on Roger, as he was consumed with his work with the Reds and therefore not able to witness Lynne's everyday actions. What he had hoped would engage her and bring her back from "too much religiosity" would instead send her even more deeply into prayer. Indeed the whole endeavor engaged her and enlivened her, but prayer was becoming her bedrock, and now even more so.

Mary Lee Tracy, now twenty-three, wasn't very interested when Lynne first asked her if she'd run the gym. The whole thing seemed half-baked to her. Lynne was a nice enough lady but knew nothing about buying or owning a gym. She had only been around gyms long enough to occasionally drop off Becky and pick her up. True, she also connected with Mary Lee in a more personal way, as they had become casual friends along the way, and they enjoyed each other's company. But that didn't qualify her to run a gym. Besides, Mary Lee had a decent coaching position already and was sorting out exactly what she wanted to do in life. She was young, and there were so many choices in front of her.

Mary Lee had been active in high school and did gymnastics as a sophomore and as a junior in order to help her cheerleading skills.

By her own admission, she wasn't much of a gymnast. But she did enjoy cheering and even spent two seasons as a Cincinnati Bengals cheerleader. All that was in the past now.

She felt like she was just getting started in life, and leaving her good coaching position in order to work for a sweet but unqualified lady didn't seem to make much sense. Beyond that, she was still sizing up Lynne. Sure, they were casual friends, but Mary Lee was uncomfortable with Lynne's deeply held spiritual convictions. The twenty-three year old was still figuring out her own spirituality, and she wasn't sure if Lynne had things right, or if Lynne was a bit "out there."

Lynne had always been good to her, and Mary Lee knew that Lynne loved how she had coached Becky when she was just a pre-schooler. Lynne could see that Mary Lee, though not in any way an accomplished gymnast, instinctively struck the perfect balance in coaching. She had high expectations and was demanding, and she was a fantastic teacher. She made everyone around her want to please her; athletes and kids around her wanted to live up to those high expectations every day. At the same time, Mary Lee treated others with respect and dignity. She never degraded anyone the way the Losantiville coach had.

> "The **way** you work with the kids is more important than the specifics of what you coach them or don't coach them."

"I just know you're the right person for this, Mary Lee," Lynne said to her as they sat in comfortable chairs near the fireplace in the neighborhood coffee shop.

"But I keep telling you I've never coached competitive gymnastics, Lynne. Sure, I like working with the kids, but what I do with the little ones is completely different than what a real coach has to do with serious athletes that are older and more skilled."

Lynne just smiled as if she didn't hear a word of Mary Lee's objection. "The *way* you work with the kids is more important than the specifics of what you coach them or don't coach them, Mary Lee. We'll be fine as long as we stay focused on treating people the right way."

"Okay, so let's just assume that's correct, Lynne. What about all the other stuff? What about managing the place? Look, I like you. You know I like you. But Lynne, what about scheduling and fees and equipment and insurance and paying bills, and managing parents who all think their little girl is the next all-star, and getting repairs done to the facility and buying foam mats and repairing equipment and... Look, Lynne, I respect you, but you don't know anything about running a gym. No offense, but I don't want to leave my current job and end up unemployed in six months because we didn't know what we were doing."

Lynne said, "I know. You're right, but I just have this feeling that it's all going to work out. Hey, what if you became an owner? You know a hundred times more than I do about running a gym."

"I've thought about that," said Mary Lee. "I'm still considering it." She looked at Lynne carefully as she said this, trying even harder to ascertain the lady she was talking to. Envoy to My Future? Or Benign Crazy Lady?

Lynne said, "Let's pray about it, Mary Lee," and they did.

...Benign Crazy Lady, Mary Lee thought to herself, as Lynne quietly prayed aloud for both of them in the coffee shop, unnoticed by the other patrons.

The Ruhl family, 1983. (L to R) Roger, Becky, Lynne (and their terrier, Bo).

CHAPTER 6

RIGHT WING HEAVY

March 30, 1983, 5:12 a.m., Newark International Airport, New Jersey

Newark Tower:	*"Central Twenty-Seven, this is Newark Approach Control. You're cleared for visual approach on runway four-right… not below two until on final."*
Central Airlines Flight 27:	*"Newark Approach Control, this is Central Twenty-Seven. Roger."*
Newark Tower:	*"Central Twenty-seven, this is Approach Control. You're cleared for landing on four-right. Winds three-hundred-forty degrees at nine knots."*
Central Airlines Flight 27:	*"Approach Control, this is Twenty-Seven. Roger. Landing on four-right. Winds three-four-zero at nine knots."*

At 5:14 a.m. Central Airlines Flight 27 touched down on runway four-right at Newark International Airport. The Learjet craft came in right-wing heavy, bounced slightly, and suddenly cart

wheeled to its right. As it tumbled, it burst into flames in the pre-dawn darkness, before finally coming to rest in the drainage ditch that separates Newark International from the New Jersey Turnpike. The only passengers, the captain and co-pilot, were both killed in the crash.

Becky's 'all-time most favorite uncle in the whole wide world' was gone. The captain was Lynne Ruhl's brother, Brad.

Lynne's mother called her to relay the horrible news. After taking the call, Lynne got in her car and drove, half out of her mind with shocked disbelief, to her parent's house. She prayed as she made her way through the early morning commuter traffic. She prayed from someplace down deep. It wasn't her that was directing the prayer, but rather it was that Inner Force that brought the words up:

"God, please give me a faith so strong that I would simply trust You when to simply trust You would be the hardest thing of all."

In that moment, in the midst of learning of her brother's horrific death, in the impersonal and isolated emptiness of an automobile, trusting God was truly the hardest thing of all for Lynne. Yet it seemed to her that God indeed answered that prayer and gave her the inexplicable faith she sought. In that horrible, tragic moment, in that searing pain and lonely bewilderment, in that terrible time when trusting God seemed the most difficult thing of all, Lynne Ruhl couldn't help but to trust God.

It seemed that on that day and with that prayer, God gave Lynne what can only be called a gift of faith. From that day forward, she found herself with a conviction that defied reason, with a faith that was stronger than logic.

She would need it to believe what was soon coming.

So would Mary Lee.

CHAPTER 7

PROMISES

Throngs came to Brad's funeral. He was a popular guy. On top of that, *The Cincinnati Enquirer* covered the tragic story in detail, and all the local news channels covered it.

Mary Lee attended, mostly as a sign of support for her grieving friend, Lynne. The funeral was a particularly moving one, largely because of Brad's general popularity and his all too soon death. He went in his absolute prime, perhaps even before it. Eulogies were delivered and hugs were shared, and all wrestled with the reality that life is indeed too short and precariously

> They wrestled with the reality that life is indeed too short and precariously uncertain.

uncertain. While everyone there was deeply touched, some were particularly moved and experienced their own faith transformations that day. Mary Lee was one. She didn't hear voices or see visions, but on that day, something deep inside her acknowledged the fundamental reality of a Maker and came to accept that life has purpose. She didn't go overboard. She didn't begin listening to Nancy Honeytree albums or praying out loud in coffee shops, but faith visited her in a different way on that day and took up residence and stayed put. Mary Lee shared this with Lynne as best as she could.

"I'm so sorry, Lynne," Mary Lee said to her grieving friend after the ceremony, as they stood outside the church.

"Oh, thank you so much for being here, Mary Lee," said Lynne.

They hugged and physically supported the collapse that felt

imminent in each of them, each wobbly-kneed supporter calling on a special reserve of strength to hold up the other.

Mary Lee said, "You're right, Lynne. I know now that you're right. About God and all – I know it. I don't know what to do about that, but I *know* it. Something happened to me today, Lynne. I believe now. I believe in a way I've never believed before."

"Oh, Mary Lee." Lynne teared up anew, mixed in grief and joy.

"But," Mary Lee said with an involuntary chuckle and a loving smile, "I still think you're a little crazy, my friend." The two women stayed in their embrace, laughed out loud and choked down tears.

"We'll talk," said Lynne. "We'll talk."

The following week they would do just that; they would talk.

Lynne was struck at how Brad's life – and especially his death – meant so much to so many people. More than she could ever have guessed. She heard from complete strangers and from people who had never even met Brad. They all told her about how their lives had been made better by her brother. Some were touched by how he had treated them, and others reported they were influenced by those Brad had influenced. In the process she came to see that, throughout the course of our lives, we touch others and make impacts that matter, though we may never see the results. She concluded that people don't have to do big, loud, noisy things to make a difference, though big things would certainly do it. Little things could make big differences too.

One week later Mary Lee sat at Lynne's kitchen table while the drip coffee maker gurgled to completion, and warm, pleasant coffee aroma filled the space around them. The negotiations to buy the gym had progressed to the point where the lawyer was relaying specifics regarding Cincinnati Gymnastics Academy: price, payment terms, transition period, ownership of receivables and payables, liability, and so forth. Lynne still wanted Mary Lee to become the coach at the gym, and Mary Lee was still reluctant, still sorting out what next steps she wanted to take. Maybe she should buy the gym herself... but how would a twenty-three year old with only very modest savings do that?

When it came to the business side of things, Lynne felt uncertain. With each passing day she became increasingly excited about the prospect of buying and owning a gymnasium. But at the same time, she was wise enough and had enough business savvy from her own years at managing pieces of the Cincinnati Reds business, that she recognized there was something in the category of "I don't know what I don't know" about embarking on this venture. By contrast, Mary Lee felt drawn like a moth to a flame. She knew it was a wildly bold step, yet there was something just irresistible about it all. And being only twenty-three, she was bold enough, and maybe even naive enough, to think she could make it work.

> Throughout the course of our lives, we touch others and make impacts that matter, though we may never see the results.

"Sometimes, Lynne," Mary Lee said, enjoying the smell of coffee in her mug but not drinking it, "I get really excited about the gym – about the idea of running it on a day-to-day basis for you. Other days, I'm not so sure. I mean, it really is a huge step for you into a brand new area. Then on other days, I want to just buy it myself and go all out. I just don't know what's right. I don't know if I should be doing any of this at all."

Lynne said, "I just know you should be doing this, Mary Lee. And I should too. But I'll admit I have second thoughts sometimes also. It's daunting, isn't it?"

Mary Lee just bit her lip and stirred her coffee endlessly.

Lynne continued, "I want to tell you something. I *need* to tell you something, Mary Lee. And it makes me nervous because I know you already think I'm a bit whacky, and this will probably make you think that even more."

Mary Lee looked squarely at Lynne, said nothing and kept

slowly stirring.

"I need to tell you what happened this morning," Lynne said with a confessionary smile. She reached into her purse and pulled out a small note pad but didn't open it. "This is going to sound crazy, I know, but that's okay. Mary Lee, I woke up this morning and even before I was truly conscious I felt this immediate, urgent, literally overwhelming need to find a paper and pen and write down this thing that was in my head... but I didn't know what 'this thing in my head' was. I just knew *something* was there and that it was incredibly important. And I knew I *had* to write it down, whatever it was. I sat up and reached over to the nightstand near my bed and got this little notebook and a pen and the words just came tumbling out. I didn't know what word was coming next, but word after word came in rapid succession, and all I did was write. I didn't think. I *couldn't* think. I just wrote. It was like the words were coming from someplace outside of me and going *through* me, and I was just putting them on paper. I didn't even have any idea what I had written until *after* I finished writing and then read it back to myself."

> She had long held a belief that if she ever "accepted" something from God, it would necessarily come with a burden. Burden, she always figured, would be part of the deal.

"Oh, my gosh," Mary Lee said, not sure if she was anxious to hear where this was going. The whole thing was giving her goose bumps. Her eyes were locked on Lynne and, irresistibly compelled, she asked, "What was it? What was the message?"

Lynne opened the manila notepad and flipped past a few pages. She found the page she wanted, took a deep breath, and tore it out. She held it in her hand as if she was handling something sacred, the way a Catholic priest holds the Eucharist, and turning her face back to Mary Lee, added one more piece to the puzzle. "Mary Lee, I know for certain that the message is for *both* you and me. I don't know *how* I know. I just know." With that, she handed the handwritten notepaper to Mary Lee:

---

1. *One day Cincinnati Gymnastics Academy will be nationally and internationally known.*

2. *One day Cincinnati Gymnastics Academy will change the way gymnastics is being trained worldwide.*

3. *One day gymnasts from around the country will be moving to Cincinnati to train. They will be thinking they are coming for good gymnastics, but we are to know they are coming here to heal.*

After reading it, Mary Lee looked up, speechless.

"There's one last thing," Lynne said. She no longer felt awkward. The discomfort had simply vanished, and now she felt a pure and gentle confidence, felt the clarity and ease that comes from absolute certainty.

Mary Lee looked at her and remained patient. Their eyes stayed locked in silence for a few long moments.

"And I knew," Lynne continued, "I knew the moment I read this to myself that it is already done."

"Oh, Lynne, you're freaking me out... What do you mean?"
Lynne's gentle but certain confidence and ease became even more manifest now, and Lynne was aware of it, even a bit surprised by it. She recognized the irony that was inside her. She recognized that she had long held a belief, not really a conscious one but a belief nevertheless, that if she ever "accepted" something from God, it would necessarily come with a burden. Burden, she always figured, would be

part of the deal. Sacrifice would always be part of the deal. Yet in this moment, with full awareness of the magnitude of this "thing" that seemed to have been placed in her lap, Lynne saw clearly that this "thing" was already done. *Done*. And she *knew* it. Burden had no part in this; burden wasn't invited; burden never entered into it. To use the Christian phrase, she felt yoked, yes. But she didn't feel burden.

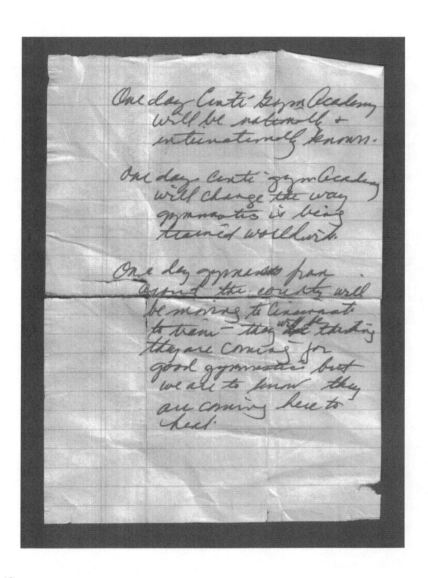

"I mean that He has already done it; He has already made those things a reality, even though they are not here yet. Cincinnati Gymnastics Academy *will* be known around the world and it *will* change how gymnastics is trained. World class gymnasts *will* come. They *will* come to be healed even though they won't know that. These three promises… they are already done."

Even though every ounce of her thought this was crazy talk, Mary Lee Tracy responded plainly and from her depths, "I know, Lynne. I know."

Mary Lee solemnly folded the paper and tucked it deep into the pages of her Bible.

A few weeks later, the final decision to buy the gym was made, and gymnastics would indeed change forever. A housewife from Fairfield, Ohio, and a twenty-three year old pre-school gymnastics teacher and ex-cheerleader would commit themselves to a sport they knew hardly anything about, and to a bunch of kids in a rundown, ramshackle gymnasium.

They'd keep quiet about the outrageous promise to make the place world famous. The whole venture was ridiculous enough without all that.

"Some of the world's greatest feats
were accomplished by people
not smart enough to know they were impossible."

Doug Larson
Author and Columnist for the Green Bay Press-Gazette

PART TWO

CULTURE FIRST

CHAPTER 8

PLACE
AND PURPOSE

The gym, the building itself, was as lowly and inadequate as the stated goals of the place were lofty and perfect.

The "gym," if it could be called that, was a converted warehouse, about sixty feet wide by eighty feet long with a ceiling about ten feet high. Years ago it had been a soda pop bottling facility, then it became a warehouse, and now it was a gym. It was sandwiched between an alley on one side and a trailer park on the other. One mobile home was planted about three feet from the wall of the "gym," which also served as the community center for the trailer park residents. It had seven parking spaces out front. The gym leaked when it rained. It got infested by bugs on a regular basis and the place had to be closed for one week each summer because of rampant termite infestations.

Original CGA home (right) with neighboring trailer (left)

One of the first tasks for the new managers, Lynne and Mary Lee, was to get the place insured. So they called and arranged for the insurance specialist to come out and inspect the place and give them a quote for coverage. A week later the insurance man arrived at Cincinnati Gymnastics Academy. He said hello and told them he had inspected eighteen gymnasiums already that year; CGA would make nineteen. After a few hours the man gave them the results. The gymnastics equipment itself – the parallel bars and vault tables and beams – were in such poor repair and had such fundamental problems that his company would not insure them. "We can't insure this equipment," he said. "We would condemn it instead." CGA's operations had been stalled before the new ownership could even get things rolling.

Beyond the bugs and leaks and uninsurable equipment, the place was simply too small to serve as an adequate training facility for competitive gymnastics. For example, there was no dimension adequate for athletes to make their approaches to the vault, which normally requires a sprint of at least eighty feet before hitting the vault table itself, and then subsequently hitting the landing area. Doing it right required at least one hundred feet of uninterrupted space. Eighty total was all they had, and to get that, they had to open a closet door along one of the walls and had vaulters start their still-too-short sprint from inside the closet. The gymnasts awaited their turn for the vault by queuing up beside the refrigerator, which stood next to the closet door.

Ten foot ceilings were insufficient. Athletes using the vault or the beam, and especially the uneven bars needed much more vertical space than that. To remedy this, some dads were recruited and set to work on a solution. They decided to cut holes in the ceiling and build elevated boxes above the new holes, which finally gave the athletes a section of ceiling fifteen feet high. They called them "doggie boxes," as they looked from the outside like overgrown doghouses situated on the roof of the place. Crews jack hammered through the concrete floor to make landing pits that would be filled with foam rubber, standard stuff in competitive gyms.

Inside CGA, "doggie box" cut into the ceiling

Example of a "foam pit," where athletes practiced landings

CGA's landing pits were filled with solid slabs of polyurethane foam (called resi-pits), sufficient to soften most landings. But they did not offer sufficient protection when CGA athletes first tried out dangerous new maneuvers and risked landing on their heads. For those occasions, CGA athletes and coaches had to travel to other gyms, in order to use their safer foam pits (see photo), which offered much better protection for an athlete landing upside down. After the athlete gained enough skill with the maneuver to not risk landing on her head, they could return to CGA for further work on that skill.

And right in the middle, exactly in the center of this completely inadequate gym, stood a ten feet wide by ten feet long walled obstruction: the bathroom. The bathroom was not in a corner. It was not along a distant wall, as it is in almost every gym in the world, and probably in almost every soda bottling operation, for that matter. No, the bathroom at CGA stood smack in the middle of the already too small facility.

It was no world class gym. It was too short, too narrow, too leaky, too bug infested, and didn't have anywhere near enough parking. And now it was sidelined, uninsurable because of inadequate equipment.

Anyone except a twenty-three year old preschool gymnastics teacher and a stay-at-home housewife with zero gymnastics experience would have folded, walked away, and cut their losses. Instead, Lynne and Mary Lee clarified what they were all about, and zeroed in on principles about how they'd operate. They had been talking about it for some time, and they were in complete agreement.

From the outset, Lynne was insistent on operating from clear principles. After all, the whole idea behind buying a gym was to do things the right way. Lynne would not subject her daughter to the ridicule, degradation, and manipulation she had witnessed in so many competitive gyms.[2] The whole idea was to do competitive gymnastics in a way that communicated to every athlete that they were respected,

---

[2] In 1995, award winning author Joan Ryan wrote the book, *Little Girls in Pretty Boxes* (published by Doubleday), a blockbuster expose of the abusive coaching practices prevalent in women's gymnastics and figure skating. The coaching mindset at the time was laced with condemnation, ridicule, and manipulation. Coaches seemed bent on creating stoic, emotion-less athletes that ignored injuries and pain, shunned food and medicine, and did exactly what they were told.

trusted, and loved. If CGA turned out good gymnasts, fine. But that would not be their goal. If they were to produce good, competitive athletes, it would be as a by-product of treating them with respect and human dignity.

"One of the great untruths out there is that people have to earn respect," Lynne said in one planning session with Mary Lee. "It's a lie. We are all born with a certain human dignity, and every one of us deserves to be respected. Not because we do anything to earn it, but because we are made by our Creator, and it is therefore a core, human condition. At this gym, we won't start from a position of 'you have to earn our respect.' We'll start from 'we respect you – period.' That doesn't mean we can't be tough. It doesn't mean we won't be demanding. It doesn't mean we won't have incredibly high standards. We will. But we'll always treat people with respect and dignity because they are endowed with those rights as human beings." Mary Lee embraced this. It wasn't that Lynne convinced her, but rather Lynne simply gave clear words to what was already bubbling inside Mary Lee.

> One of the great untruths out there is that people have to earn respect.
> We are born with human dignity, and as such, everyone deserves basic respect. It is a condition of being human. It is a fundamental right that comes from our Maker.

The next day they hung a large sign on the wall inside CGA, in clear view for all to see:

I can do all this through Him who strengthens me.
Phil 4:13

They also agreed on a simple, unofficial statement that summed up what they wanted to be all about: *"Good gymnastics done fun."* This sentence and the sign on the wall said everything.

Lynne and Mary Lee were just inexperienced enough, just naïve enough to believe they could have it both ways. They were just idealistic enough to think they could treat everyone with respect and dignity AND get great results. And if they couldn't have it both ways, they were clear on which part took priority: the part about dignity and respect.

The principles were clear. The sign on the wall looked great. All they needed now was to get the leaking, bug-infested, poorly equipped, ridiculously substandard gym operating again.

> "To believe in something, and not to live it, is dishonest."
>
> *M. K. Gandhi*

CHAPTER 9

FAMILY FIRST

They did just that; they got the place operating again, finally. In the short term they literally duct-taped equipment to make it serviceable enough to safely use. Longer term, and after further investment, they repaired and replaced equipment. Gymnastics sessions began in earnest. But it seemed that as soon as they solved one problem, another one surfaced.

A financial analysis suggested that their current enrollment of about two hundred girls was woefully insufficient; they would need to more than triple the number of athletes to make ends meet.

In a strange way they were lucky the problem was so big. Had the gap been smaller, they might have tried all the "normal" things any business person would do to increase revenues. But in the face of such a daunting challenge, they decided to simply stick to their principles and just do the right thing: good gymnastics done fun. Rather than launching an enrollment campaign, they decided to launch a "fun" campaign. But what would "fun" look like for young girls?

One notable example is the campaign they aimed at Valentines' Day, that magical day which rivals all others in the lives of school aged girls. Coaches and staffers studied the girls' performances and placed red hearts on the floor where their feet should hit on certain floor exercises. They marked off pacing distances on the beam with heart-shaped stickers and placed them at the beginning of the girls' vault runs. When one girl struggled with a giant swing on the bars and failed to extend her legs fully when rotating her legs past the low bar, they placed a heart-shaped card on the floor mat and encouraged her to tap it with her toes as they swung by. Accomplishments were rewarded with a small box of raisins, hair barrettes, face paints, or "Good Job!" stickers. The kids loved it and had fun as they improved.

They instituted "Gym Bucks," a program in which positive, kind acts were recognized and rewarded with gym bucks, their own, distinct version of Monopoly money. When a coach overheard one gymnast encouraging another, she was rewarded with gym bucks, which could later be cashed in for prizes like embroidered CGA sweatshirts or CGA-branded leotards. The bigger prizes included Sony Walkmans, Peppermint Patty moppets, or Atari Mario Brothers games. Things eventually evolved to where one girl could reward another by allotting a certain amount of gym bucks when her peer demonstrated kindness or a positive attitude. One day, eleven year old Mary Ellen Miller spotted ten year old Kris Cahill ushering preschoolers out of harm's way when they wandered too close to one athlete's floor exercise. Mary Ellen awarded five gym bucks to Kris on the spot. And an observing coach immediately awarded ten to Mary Ellen for reinforcing Kris's good behavior.

They arranged sleepovers at the gym and ordered pizza and organized "The Price is Right" games, complete with Mary Lee playing the "Come on down!" role of Bob Barker. The kids competed in the games, laughed, ate, and collapsed in sleeping bags or blankets as they sprawled on gym mats or in the foam padded landing pits. They had Fourth of July themes, Halloween programs, and they celebrated birthdays. Exceptionally good performances – and good attitudes – sometimes earned the hard working athlete a day off, complete with a few coaches and staffers taking the girl out for a ladies' day at the spa.

The approach was deliberate. It was intentional. These weren't just willy-nilly, feel-good celebrations. Each event, each competition, each spa trip and each gym-bucks transaction created a unique teaching opportunity, and the CGA coaches used those opportunities to the fullest. They stated and restated what they wanted: good gymnastics done fun. With each ex-change, they rein-forced the belief that CGA would do both – both fun *and* good

> Why are you leading? Is it to serve or to be served? Answering this question in a truthful way is so important. You can't fake being a servant leader.
>
> Ken Blanchard
> *Leading at a Higher Level*

gymnastics, and that *everyone* deserved respect and dignity. They reinforced the values of discipline and positive attitude, of hard work and persistence. And most of all, excellence. Always excellence. And the kids responded.

During this same time period, they instituted regular Bible Study and Sports Psychology classes. They worked on the entire person, the whole athlete. Their focus extended far beyond the physical. The athlete, after all, was a *person*.

Lynne led Bible Study sessions and gently introduced the kids to biblical principles, like giving dignity, practicing unity, treating others as you would have them treat you, praying, and most of all, evangelizing by practicing their beliefs, by "living it out." Kids of other, non-Christian faiths were invited, never pressured to join. They always did. The group always started with prayer and Scripture, but each class quickly evolved into practical discussions of how the concept or principle played out in their everyday lives. By setting the example, by practicing true servant leadership, Lynne and other staffers shared from the heart and in so doing, made themselves vulnerable. More importantly, these courageous steps made Bible Study a safe place for all, and the conversations began to flow freely.

The kids were starting to come around.

But the parents, it seemed, fought them every step of the way during those early months.

Inside CGA – bathroom in the middle of the gym floor.

CHAPTER 10

TOXICITY
AND PUSHBACK

"But I run the schedule; I *own* the schedule! I've been doing this at CGA for three years. I've got two kids in this program, don't forget – *two* kids. And I know how to run the schedule so it works for most families here." Deb Holleran[3], mother of two competitive CGA gymnasts, didn't like the idea of turning the scheduling responsibilities over to Mary Lee and Lynne. Scheduling had become part of Deb's routine and part of her identity in a way, and doing it allowed her to exercise some control over things at CGA. "You think you can do better, well good luck, lady..." She slapped the scheduling spreadsheet on the table and walked out. Deb hoped they'd fail. When they published a schedule that conflicted with the school's Spring Festival Day – and Deb knew they would – Deb would lead a clandestine revolt. She'd work through back channels and encourage other parents to prioritize the festival over gymnastics. See how they like a half-empty gym. She'd do her best to make sure these new

---

[3] Other than Lynne Ruhl and Mary Lee Tracy, all the names in this chapter are fictitious. The events themselves are real.

"bosses," who were taking scheduling duties away from her, learned their lesson.

Deb Holleran wasn't alone. Tina McGee, another gym mom, ran the toddlers' program, and Gail Emmit owned finances. Elsa Brande, Minnie Collier, and Gary and Jessica Halverford all owned their pieces. And they all resented giving up the power they had previously enjoyed. It had been "their" gym, after all. They had set the tone. They had decided what meets to compete in, which kids would participate in what events, and who would have keys to the place. Some of them even "coached." None of them liked the changes. None of them liked the order, the operating discipline, the new meritocracy that was being installed. While a few of them drew a modest stipend for their contributions, most freely gave their time and effort to CGA. The unstated deal, the unofficial return was the exercise of power, the ability to control. Their girls got special treatment, sure, but weren't they entitled to that, given all they did for CGA?

But all that was now changing.

There were more than a few incidents of sabotage during that first year. Resentful parents, newly stripped of their power to run CGA their way, conveniently forgot to attend certain CGA events and to pass key information along to others. They invented ways to misinterpret dress code rules and travel plans for important meets. One parent hid the leotard belonging to a gymnast who was to compete against her daughter, just before the coaches were to evaluate the two girls and place one of them in an upcoming meet. Another parent suddenly "had trouble with her bank account," and couldn't figure out why the bank was preventing her from paying her CGA dues. Things got even worse when a few competitive athletes who previously enjoyed the benefits of favoritism had to compete head-to-head with other, more talented gymnasts. Judges' scores now reflected performance on the floor rather than clubby preference.

Resentful parents booed the performances of girls competing against their daughters. They visited other gyms and openly threatened to leave CGA – and to take others with them if they could. Bad behavior fed on bad behavior, like a stubborn virus that refused to leave. It seemed things were getting worse, not better.

Lynne and Mary Lee stayed the course. They gradually brought the operation under their control and continued making changes that reflected their beliefs, all the while treating others with dignity and respect, even when they themselves were facing attacks and ridicule. They stayed on the high road when resentful parents challenged their approach.

Those first months were particularly tough on the new management at CGA. They would have to find a way to better engage the parents and family, to replace the toxicity there with something better. It would be another few months until they found a constructive way to do that.

CGA gymnasts on beam

CHAPTER 11

EXCELLENCE

Mary Lee Tracy was (and is) more than special. She had a gift for coaching that couldn't be missed; it was so natural and obvious to anyone who looked. She was charismatic. She was smart. She was determined. She had high expectations – of athletes, of staff, and especially of herself. And she was absolutely, unequivocally, positively committed to excellence. She was so committed to excellence that she would not allow anything to get in the way. Not even herself.

The twenty-three year old Mary Lee studied everything she could get her hands on regarding how to coach gymnastics. Her appetite for learning gymnastics was insatiable. She visited other gyms, asked thousands of questions, read books and articles and watched videos. She consumed everything she could get her hands on. And she never let her ego get in the way by shying away from asking one more question, even if her asking might have made her look inadequate. Her image didn't matter to her. The degree to which she was perceived as the expert – or not the expert – didn't matter to her. Her own comfort didn't matter to her. Excellence mattered. Excellence was all that mattered.

When Brandi Ashworth, one of CGA's better athletes, needed to learn a double flip dismount from the uneven bars, Mary Lee called another gym with a strong reputation, asked if one of their coaches would teach her how to spot the dangerous maneuver, and travelled a long distance to learn the skills she needed to coach Brandi. She arrived at the competitive gym, walked right in, and said, "I don't know how to spot this skill, would you please teach me?" Because that's what you do when you are committed to excellence. One week later, Brandi was double-flipping at CGA while Mary Lee spotted her.

Mary Lee imbedded passion for excellence into everything that happened at CGA. With only a few exceptions, the majority of CGA girls were simply not yet competitive gymnasts. They couldn't yet perform routines difficult enough to earn competitive scores at meets. But that didn't stop Mary Lee, and by extension CGA, from pursuing absolute excellence. "Maybe it's true," she told her athletes, "that you can't yet perform degrees of difficulty that will earn you top scores. But one day you're going to. And today, right now, even though you can't do those difficult routines, there *are* things you can do with excellence. And we're going to do *everything* with excellence. Excellence is an attitude. It's a *choice*. Excellence is a habit, and it starts here. It starts now."

And so CGA gymnasts learned basic things, like toe-points, and did them over and over and over, until they performed them perfectly. They broke difficult moves into their simplest component pieces, called 'progressions,' and worked on each element, each progression, until they performed that portion of the move with absolute excellence. Most of all, they focused on not having any execution errors and performing each move cleanly. They didn't focus on tackling difficult routines and maneuvers; they focused on perfect executions, even if that meant sticking to simple routines.

"We can't do double back flips yet, but we can do clean progressions, and we can have zero execution errors. We can do toe-points, and we can have perfectly straight legs. We can be totally clean in everything we do!" Mary Lee coached her athletes to achieve excellence where they could, and to settle for nothing less than absolute excellence. They prepared for meets with excellence. They tied their hair back with excellence, entered the gym with excellence, stretched and warmed up as a team with excellence, marched as a team from event to event with excellence, walked off the floor after their routines with excellence, and even wore their uniforms with remarkable attention to detail – and above all, excellence.

Mary Lee would often host groups of athletes at her house on evenings or weekends. She'd feed them healthy snacks, and they'd watch gymnastics videos in her living room, breaking down basic moves they were trying to master in the gym. Mary Lee would talk them through a specific part of the maneuver that played on the screen, and then they'd slow it down and study it frame by frame, over and over. They came to expect excellence in the smallest of things.

When the team travelled, there were expectations, rules of behavior that spelled out excellence in relationships and team behavior. There were expectations about where they slept, what they ate, how they behaved in public and in private, about appearance, courtesy, and about behavior in hotel hallways and lobbies. There were expectations about how they interacted with one another, about how they were to behave as team, throughout the entire trip. Here's just one example, handwritten by Mary Lee, to three CGA athletes who were to travel to one particular meet in Reno:

"To: The Chosen Three
From: The Boss

The Reno Rules
1. *Stick together like glue. You are a threesome wherever you go; no one is ever to be left out or left behind.*
2. *You are a TEAM, which means you work together at everything you do. Be sensitive to each others' needs. Remember: Do unto others as you would have them do unto you.*
3. *Whispering is RUDE and forbidden – NO secrets!*
4. *If you don't have anything nice to say, don't say anything at all.*
5. *Think of Paula. Why does everyone like her so much? Because she cares about everyone and doesn't like to see anyone hurt."*

TO: The Chosen Three
FROM: The Boss

THE RENO RULES

1. Stick together like glue, you are a threesome wherever you go no one is ever to be left behind or left out.
2. You are a team which means you work together at everything you do. Be sensative to each others needs. Remember to do unto each other as you would have them do unto you.
3. Whispering is RUDE and forbidden, NO secrets!
4. If you don't have anything nice to say, don't say anything at all.
5. Third of Paula, why does everyone like her so much? Because she cares about everyone and doesn't like to see anyone hurt.

The summersaults and giant swings and spectacular vaults would come later. Excellence started on day one. Excellence was everywhere. Excellence became a habit. They came to expect it of themselves. And they came to expect it of each other.

CHAPTER 12

LISTENING
& RESPECT

"How are we supposed to treat one another?" Lynne asked the kids in her Bible Study group, singing the question more than saying it.

"With respect and dignity!" they shouted back in a single, collective voice, responding in back-and-forth, sing-song rhythm to the musical question.

"Why?"

"Because everyone deserves it!" The repetitive lessons were sinking in. It was a lighthearted recital they had come to truly enjoy.

"And why do they deserve it?"

"Because they're HUMAN!" The girls loved hitting the high note on 'human;' it was their fully sanctioned, fully authorized opportunity to scream something at the top of their lungs. They belted it out in unison, and they loved it.

"And how do we *show* people how much we respect them?"

Their reciprocating song, their jovial, rhythmic question and answer slowed to an awkward stop with this question – it was a new one, and the girls had no answer for it. There was a long moment of puzzled silence. A single hand finally shot up. "We show it by *telling* the person that we respect them?" The girl presented her words as a question, not an answer.

"Good idea. There's a better way. Anybody else?" Lynne asked, searching the young faces for eyes that had a different answer.

"We show our respect for people by letting them go in front of us in line?"

Lynne said, "Those are good things, but that's not the best way to show people we respect them. The best way for us to respect people, the way that makes people *know* they are being respected, is by *listening* to them. Does that make sense to you? Think about how you interact with your friends and family. When you feel listened to – really listened to – do you feel respected? Compare how you feel when somebody is really listening to you, with how you feel when somebody says 'I respect you' but doesn't really listen…"

Another hand shot up and Lynne nodded to the girl. "Dad always says how much he respects my mom, but when they're talking I can tell he doesn't listen, and I know it hurts Mom's feelings. But she never says it."

Another hand popped up. "Yeah, Chris is my best friend and I know she respects me. I guess I like her so much because she's such a great listener."

As the session unfolded, Lynne shared more about respect and about how listening is the single most important way to demonstrate respect – and suggested that maybe it's the only way that real respect is ever communicated. She talked about how we all think we know how to listen, but the truth is we don't really know how until somebody teaches us. Listening, she told the kids, is not a natural thing for us humans. It's a learned skill, and it takes practice. She coached them on words to use and made them aware of body language, and how the body can say things without words. They broke into pairs and practiced their listening skills. The kids ate it up.

These sessions continued over those early months at CGA. Lynne emphasized listening above all other skills, and preached about the power of effective listening. She pointed out how listening – that is respect – had to come first; and how once respect is established, we can then build trust with one another. We build trust by being true to our word, by doing what we say we'll do, over and over. And after we have respect and trust, people can challenge and confront one another in ways that are healthy, and in ways that work. "And that," she told them, "means we can tackle anything; we can do anything. *Anything...*"

She taught listening skills, and later trust skills, to both the athletes and CGA staff members. Over time, the lessons permeated their everyday behaviors, and genuine respect gained a toehold in the practical lives of everyone at CGA. Respect wasn't just a word or a tagline that got recited in Bible Study. It was becoming real, and CGA began slowly transforming itself from the inside.

****

Three months later, a group of four parents, all with athletes enrolled at CGA, knocked on Lynne's modest office door. Lynne looked up and saw the faces; they looked resolute. Deep inside Lynne cringed. These were some of the unofficial ringleaders of discontent. Deb Holleran was the one who knocked, and she appeared to be their appointed spokesperson. Gail Emmit was there, the Halverfords stood behind Gail. 'What now?' Lynne thought to herself as she swallowed hard and invited them in. They declined and stood where they were, as if their heels were welded in place.

Deb spoke first. "We don't know what you're teaching our kids in Bible Study." Deb glanced at the others, nodding affirmatively as she did, signaling that what she was about to say was coming from all of them. "But our kids are behaving differently. At home, I mean. They're... they're just better, and we like it. It's making our families better. And well, whatever you're teaching them – would you be willing to teach it to us parents also?"

Tears welled up in Lynne Ruhl's eyes. She couldn't help herself, couldn't hold it back, and the tears poured down her cheeks. Lynne stood and hugged Deb Holleran, Queen of Anger and CGA Saboteur, and in soft sobs of relief, said, "You bet I will, Deb. You bet I will."

Sleepover party at CGA

CHAPTER 13

BREAKTHROUGH: TRUST

Lynne always started Bible Study sessions with a prayer and passage from Scripture before opening things up for discussion. The kids were passive at first. They were cautious, tentative, and unsure about how open they should be. But time and consistency worked its magic and brought about a certain level of comfort which eventually had the kids trusting and sharing more openly. Listening was Lynne's secret weapon. She understood that people would solve most problems themselves if they felt respected and trusted, and she understood that skillful listening was the key to communicating respect. She had taught them that, and she had taught them *how* to listen.

At the same time, familiarity and trust were being developed outside of Bible Study, because CGA coaches and staff were spending so many hours with the kids. In addition to the hours of practice, there were pizza parties, sleepovers, traveling to competitive meets, and staying in hotels. Coaches and staffers were there when the girls experienced the first stages of puberty, when they first had to deal with spotting and periods and shopping for their first bra. They were there for discussions about the awkwardness of adolescence and school friendships and academic pressures and family issues – and boys. It was a natural part of having dozens of coming-of-age girls in

> To listen well
> is as powerful a means of influence
> as to talk well.
>
> Chinese Proverb

close proximity with coaches and staffers for hours, weeks, months, and years. Familiarity and time and behaviors that consistently matched words led to trust. And trust led to open communications. While this was the norm at CGA, it took on a special level of significance in Bible Study, where trust and meaning were more profound than ever.

"So what does it mean to you?" asked Lynne, Bible Study leader, to the twenty girls who had collected around her for the forty-five minute session. She had just read them 1 Corinthians 6: 19-20 and a second one from 1 Corinthians 3: 16-17.

> *"Or do you not know that your body is a temple of the Holy Spirit within you, whom you have from God? You are not your own, for you were bought with a price. So glorify God in your body."*

> *"Do you not know that you are God's temple and that God's Spirit dwells in you? If anyone destroys God's temple, God will destroy him. For God's temple is holy, and you are that temple."*

"What does that mean to you?" Lynne repeated.

One girl immediately popped her arm up and began answering out loud, before Lynne actually called on her. "To me it means that God gave me gymnastics talent, and I'm supposed to use that talent because my body is God's more than it is mine."

Another voice chimed in. "It means that my body is sacred, and I need to treat it right – like not eating junk food but eating good stuff."

A third girl waited patiently with her arm up, and Lynne called on her. "Amy, what do you think?"

"I think it means that it's not me doing a giant swing out there," she pointed toward the gym floor and the uneven bars. "It's God doing it through my body."

The discussion went on like this for a few minutes before things slowed down a bit. It was clear to Lynne that the group was getting the idea and that despite their young ages, the girls were grasping how this passage applied in real life. She was about to move on to the next passage she had preselected, but before she could, Katie Miller interrupted her.

"Lynne?" Katie asked, her arm held high.

"What is it, Katie?" Lynne asked of the twelve year old.

"I also think it means we can't commit murder… or suicide."

Lynne was a bit surprised at the directness of the awkward topic but quickly decided to embrace it. After all, it was one of the girls that brought it up.

"I agree, Katie. That's exactly right." Lynne watched the faces and saw one set of eyes turn down.

"I think about suicide sometimes," said the girl without looking up and without waiting her turn. "I mean I'm just saying…"

"Me too," came from another girl in the back row, but Melissa said it directly and without shame, flatly, matter of factly, looking right at Lynne as she spoke. "I know it's not right, and it's not like I'm really going to do it, but I admit I think about it sometimes."

And with that, the flood gates opened and adolescent girls bubbled up with confessions of self doubt and the occasional self loathing that afflicts young people. They discussed the melancholy and despondency that has become, or maybe has always been, part of the growing up process. Together they wrestled with the sad life stage that seemed like a rite of passage for so many young people. And suicide too. It was out there now; it had been named; it was in the daylight. And in exposing the thing, they vanquished it. It seemed so much smaller and less frightening once they called it out, rolled it around and examined the thing together.

It brought up the topic of fear. They talked of fear of parents, school, the future, boys, and yes, gymnastics.

Jackie Miles, one of the gym's better athletes, confessed to her fear of performing a difficult pre-flight portion of her vault routine. The maneuver called for a sprint followed by a round-off to the springboard and then a handspring onto the vault table. She had no trouble with the round-off, but the handspring unnerved her. The handspring onto the vault table caused her to freeze up in fear. It was dangerous and difficult, and Jackie knew that at full speed, she could get seriously hurt. Her coaches had worked her through the progressions, through all the elements of the maneuver, and she performed each individual element with excellence. All she had to do was string it all together. But Jackie feared it. She feared failing and feared injury and feared being afraid. And now she admitted all this openly to her peers and coaches.

"I can do it; I know I'm capable of doing it – I'm just afraid. I'm scared. I'm really afraid of trying it."

One by one the girls began to rally around Jackie. As it became increasingly clear that the issue was not skill or preparation, that the issue was simply and exclusively fear, they offered support. And they did more than that – they thrust their support on her.

"I watched you practicing all the elements, Jackie – you were nailing it!"

"I know you can do it, Jackie. Remember how you were kind of afraid of doing your first full-twisting dismount, too, and you nailed that one, stuck the landing first time. I mean, girl, you *stuck* it!"

A chorus of unplanned, genuine support erupted, a full and spontaneous symphony of voices. "We're with you, Jackie!" and "You can do it – I *know* you can do it!" They had risen to their feet and surrounded their peer. They clapped and patted her back and cheered her on. The outburst was so heartfelt and so genuine that Lynne marveled at the spirit in the group and simply stood back and watched. The rousing, cheering rabble literally surrounded Jackie and paraded her out to the gym floor, and in so doing stifled all the activity that had been going on there. Coaches stood back and staffers stepped aside, while every athlete in the building was drawn straight into the scene. This was solely the girls' act, their part in the unfolding drama of CGA, and somehow everybody in the building instantly grasped that unspoken truth.

"You can do it Jackie! We're with you! We're right here."

Surrounded by unrestrained loving support, by raw selfless encouragement, and even by challenge rooted in respect and trust, Jackie Miles took up her position in that closet… that humble, modest storage closet that was the ridiculous launching point for a vault sprint. She took in the voices and eyes around her, narrowed her focus, and blasted off forcefully and with the determination of an entire team. She streaked toward the springboard, and as she got closer, the voices dwindled toward tense, time-frozen silence. Jackie hit her round-off beautifully, and hit her handspring onto the springboard without a hitch – then soared to the vault and finished her flight, collapsing in relief and gratitude as she landed in the soft foam pit. The entire place erupted. Jackie leapt up in sheer triumph and the girls swarmed her in the pit, screeching and hooraying and applauding her courage and her success.

Alone in the corner of the gym, Lynne Ruhl stood with Mary Lee Tracy and took it all in. They made eye contact with one another and smiles burst forth from them both, but neither said a word. They didn't have to. It was so obvious. The girls were getting it. They were becoming "team." Respect, trust, challenge, excellence. It was all starting to happen.

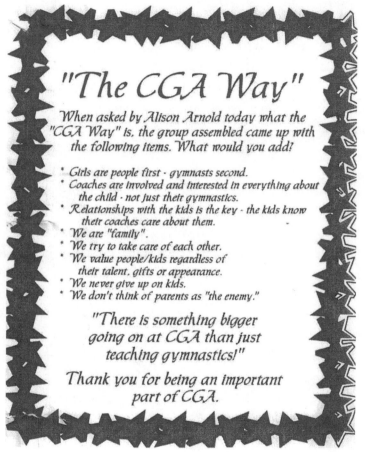

"The CGA Way"

When asked by Alison Arnold today what the "CGA Way" is, the group assembled came up with the following items. What would you add?

* Girls are people first - gymnasts second.
* Coaches are involved and interested in everything about the child - not just their gymnastics.
* Relationships with the kids is the key - the kids know their coaches care about them.
* We are "family".
* We try to take care of each other.
* We value people/kids regardless of their talent, gifts or appearance.
* We never give up on kids.
* We don't think of parents as "the enemy."

"There is something bigger going on at CGA than just teaching gymnastics!"

Thank you for being an important part of CGA.

Posted in CGA and shared with staff, athletes, and families

CHAPTER 14

BEING WHO
SHE COULD BE

Just as Mary Lee had taught herself how to be a head gymnastics coach, Lynne had taught herself how to coach athletes on the beam. She volunteered to help at meets and then paid special attention to the scoring of various events. Soon after she committed herself to learning how points were assigned – or deducted, as the sport's rules specify. She wanted to coach, she had decided. But she needed credibility first. She needed to learn her stuff. She knew she needed to earn that. She reasoned that walking in the shoes of a gymnastics judge, knowing precisely what judges looked for and how scoring was decided, would be excellent preparation for becoming a coach. So Lynne Ruhl, stay-at-home-mom and gymnastics enthusiast decided to pursue certification as a gymnastics judge.

> Start by doing what's necessary; then do what's possible; and suddenly you are doing the impossible.
>
> Francis of Assisi

She was faced with a choice. The first option was to pursue certification in judging compulsories. Compulsories are mandatory, standardized routines that every competitive athlete has to perform. And every single athlete does exactly the same routine, so judges always know precisely what's coming next; they know exactly what to look for at every moment in the routine; they can directly compare one athlete to the other.

By contrast, an "Optional Judge" must score routines that are distinct and individualized, routines each athlete makes up just for themselves. Therefore the Optional Judge has to learn *all* the possible skills and all the conceivable combinations. During an athlete's routine, the judge never knows what's coming next. For every skill, every maneuver, the judge needs to know exactly what to look for and how points are assigned – or withdrawn – for that particular skill.

> What self-imposed obstacles have I placed in my life? What is it I've told myself I cannot do?
>
> What have I told others *they* cannot do?

Not surprisingly, all Optional Judges were first Compulsory Judges. At least until Lynne came along. Being naive, she decided to pursue certification as an Optional Judge right out of the gate. Didn't she know that couldn't be done; that it was beyond reach?

A few months later, Lynne Ruhl became Region V's first certified Optional Judge who wasn't first a Compulsory Judge. Lynne, like each CGA athlete, was becoming who she was capable of becoming.

CHAPTER 15

TOUGH STUFF
& THE C.G.A. WAY

*"There is something bigger going on at CGA
than just teaching gymnastics"*

Fifteen year old Sarah had been showing promise on the beam. Lynne studied Sarah trying to figure out where the flaw was, because it was certain one had recently developed. Sarah's movements just weren't as smooth as they had been even a couple of weeks ago. But why? Lynne, the judge-turned-beam-coach, couldn't figure out what was going on with Sarah, but she was determined to identify the problem and help Sarah overcome it.

Sarah took a break and headed for the bathroom in the middle of the gym, and Lynne used that as an opportunity to go over the beam routine again in her mind, to confirm the proper rhythm and pacing of it. When she returned from the bathroom, Sarah's expression showed signs of frustration with her beam exercise, so Lynne suggested she work on the floor routine for a while instead. Lynne watched Sarah as she did her floor warm ups and practiced her routine. Something seemed off, but just as on the beam, Lynne couldn't pinpoint the problem. Sarah seemed tentative in her tumbling and seemed to lack her usual vigorous energy when she snapped into her various poses. She finished the routine and placed her hands on the small of her back, as if she was a bit winded, as if the muscles in her lower back had been taxed too much.

Sarah drifted to the uneven bars next, and Lynne kept her attentive vigil, searching for clues and insight that would help her coach Sarah when she returned to the beam. The athlete assumed her starting position near the lower bar, again with a posture that seemed

75

just slightly less than that of her usual peppy one. She reached the bar and began swinging, kicked her legs forward and up to gain momentum. She was preparing for the part of her routine in which she'd release the lower bar and grasp the upper bar, where she'd swing more forcefully before bellying the lower bar and bouncing back. Then Sarah stopped and let go, somehow dissatisfied with something in the early part of her bars routine, took a short walk and prepared to start again.

Suddenly, Lynne started her sprint toward Sarah, toward the bars before she even knew why she was sprinting. Something inside her had intuitively connected the dots and solved the mysterious puzzle before her conscious brain could catch up. "Sarah!" She called to the sixteen year old girl. "Sarah, stop! Don't mount those bars!"

The girl just stood and gawked at the beam coach sprinting in her direction. "What?" she asked, taken aback by the idea that her beam coach apparently had something dramatic to tell her about bars, a bit bewildered at the sight of a coach scooting directly toward her, and fast. It only took a couple of seconds for Lynne to arrive, and when she did, she merely took Sarah's hand and said, "Come with me."

Lynne led the athlete to her office and closed the door, sat the bewildered Sarah in a folding chair and said with her eyes that she was there for the girl. Sarah had no idea she needed Lynne's support.

"Sarah, sweetie," Lynne said with gentleness and sweetness and all the 'I'm on your side' that she could put into her tone of voice. "Honey, how are you?"

"I'm okay," Sarah said, clearly uncomfortable with being pulled off the floor and led to a private office. "I know I'm off on my routines, but I guess I'm tired is all. I just need to get more sleep, I guess."

Lynne asked, "Sarah, tell me about how things are going outside of here, outside of the gym, in the rest of your life – you know, school, parents, boys, and friends."

Sarah's expression turned to concern and befuddlement. "What's going on? I mean things are fine, I suppose. It's no big deal, really; I'll put a little more energy into my routines. Am I in trouble?"

"No honey, you're not in any trouble," Lynne said with a smile. "You never had a boyfriend before, Sarah. I know you shared that in Bible Study a few weeks ago, but, well, do you have one now?"

"Huh?" asked Sarah, still not following. "Well, no, not really. I sort of like Bobby, though. But I wouldn't call him a boyfriend, not yet anyway."

"I like you a lot, kiddo, and I respect you so much. You know that. And when I observed you out there today, I saw a young woman who went to the bathroom more than she normally does, who looks like she's a little bit tired, who might have a little tenderness in her breasts, who might have a tiny bit of back pain... Sarah, I can't help but wonder if you're pregnant..."

The teenager just stared back at Lynne, and in that moment, appeared more scared than confident, more adolescent than young woman. "But I just told you I don't have a boyfriend. I've never had a boyfriend."

"But is it possible – just possible that you might be pregnant, Sarah?"

There was full five seconds of long silence before Sarah answered. "I suppose it's possible," Sarah said, looking down at the floor rather than at her beam coach. "But it was only one time," and she began to cry softly. Lynne stood and held her and whispered that it would be okay, told her that they'd find out for sure and that Sarah wouldn't be alone in this, no matter what.

The next day Sarah took a pregnancy test, and when the results came back positive, Lynne sat and talked with her for hours. They talked about choices in life, about those choices that are behind us and those that in front of us. They talked about courage and compassion and pros and cons of various possible paths. And most of all, they talked about how Sarah would share this news with her parents. They actually role-played it a few times, with Lynne playing the part of the parents and Sarah being Sarah, trying different deliveries until she found the one that felt most honest and true.

The beam coach did exactly what she committed to doing when all this started. She loved and respected and supported the athlete in front of her. She cared for her. She remembered that the whole idea of CGA was to treat the athletes with dignity and respect and love. She recalled the idea that if they turned out great athletes, great. But that the bigger goal wasn't athletic success. She recalled the CGA Way:

The CGA Way

- *Girls are people first, gymnasts second.*
- *Coaches are involved and interested in everything about the child, not just their gymnastics.*
- *Relationships with the kids is the key – the kids know their coaches care about them.*
- *We are 'family.'*
- *We try to take care of each other.*
- *We value people/kids regardless of their talent, gifts or appearance.*
- *We never give up on kids.*
- *We don't think of parents as 'the enemy.'*

"There is something bigger going on at CGA than just teaching gymnastics!"

Thank you for being an important part of CGA.

Sarah delivered the baby. Sarah did not become a great gymnast. She became a great person.

CHAPTER 16

A CULTURE
TAKES ROOT

The months went by, and the quality of CGA gymnastics slowly improved. Lynne and Mary Lee stayed true to their principles and worked hard at "good gymnastics done fun." Parents and families took listening classes, and changes in behavior were showing up, sometimes in subtle ways and sometimes in big ones. Kids studied Scripture, explored how it was relevant to their lives, and practiced profound respect by listening skillfully. As they felt more respected, trust grew. And as trust grew, they were able to speak truth in love, sometimes holding each other accountable in ways that hadn't been possible before. The culture was changing, that much was clear.

At the same time, and without any exceptional promotions or campaigns, CGA's enrollment grew. Without focusing on the surface-level problem of numbers and enrollment, it was being solved; in fact the problem was solving itself. A steady stream of families with aspiring daughter-athletes had begun to arrive at their gym. New members were drawn by energy and attitude, by principles and passion. They were attracted not by performance on the floor, which was still sub-par for a competitive gym, but by leadership that called out the best in people.

One day Lynne got confirmation that the culture really had taken root. Again, it came in the most unlikely of ways.

Lynne was sitting on the toilet in the rest room, secluded behind a closed stall door, when she heard the restroom door burst open and heard the girls come in, bubbling with chatter as only young girls can. They were absorbed in their own conversation, and it was obvious they had no idea Lynne was there and could hear every word. It only took a moment for Lynne to realize the group consisted of two CGA girls showing the place to a prospective athlete, somebody who was considering joining CGA.

"And this," one of the CGA girls said with a proud but self-mocking flourish, "is our glamorous restroom."

"Yep. This is where it all begins," said the other CGA athlete. That's my locker right there and that's where I donned my leotard an hour ago. This room is where we get ready and where we get our game faces on. A *lot* goes on in here, as you might imagine." And with that both CGA girls giggled knowingly.

"Oh man," the newcomer chimed in, trying to insert herself into the sisterhood. "That tubby girl you just introduced me to? Stephanie? It must be something to watch her try to wiggle her blubber into those tights in here! Right?" She let out a hooting laugh that invited the other two to join in.

There was an awkward, clumsy pause, and Lynne cringed in her private cocoon, cloistered and imprisoned where she was unable to intervene. She ached for poor Stephanie, a good kid and a hard working athlete who was talented but who was a bit heavy. Darned girls can be so catty, she thought to herself. And she ached too, for the two CGA girls who knew better but were nevertheless subject to peer pressure and would be tempted to join into the pettiness.

> Once a culture is established, it sustains itself.

That's when they lifted her. That's when they made her tear up in pride. That's when she learned, when she came to *know*, that once a culture is set it sustains itself.

"I used to talk that way too," said the first CGA girl. "I did it all the time when I first got here. But you might as well know right now that we don't talk that way around here."

"That's right," the second CGA athlete added. "We just don't do it. So if you want to be here, you might as well just stop talking that way right now; nobody is going to listen." It was followed with silence. After a few long seconds, the CGA girl continued in a sing-song sort of voice, "So, come on, let's show you the offices!" and the restroom door burst open again, the girls walked out, and the sounds of the gym flooded in. And Lynne Ruhl, filled to tears with pride, sat alone in a lowly bathroom stall and pumped her fist in fierce triumph.

The culture had arrived.

Gymnastics would follow.

Inside CGA. Note the "doggie box" over the beam.

PART THREE

RESULTS WILL FOLLOW

CHAPTER 17

THE MUSE

It didn't take anyone long to see she was the best athlete in the gym. You could just sit in the stands and watch for ten minutes and sure enough, your eyes would be drawn to the girl who was just a step faster and soared just a bit higher. You'd have been unable to resist watching the girl who seemed to have just a bit more spring in her legs than anyone else in the building. Tracie Halstead had potential; that much was clear. Lynne and Mary Lee both noticed it right away.

It was in those very first days that Mary Lee said to Lynne, "Oh my gosh, that kid's got talent. She's got real potential."

Lynne said, "She sure does." But neither Lynne nor Mary Lee knew how much; they weren't calibrated yet.

Mary Lee's eyes stayed on the energetic athlete who sprinted across the floor and executed a very clean round off and back handspring. "I owe it to her to grow my own skills and knowledge, so I can help her get to wherever she's capable of going. I owe it to her to become the coach that she needs. I've got some real work to do."

In a sense, Tracie Halstead became Mary Lee's muse. She was the initial inspiration, not that Mary Lee needed it. But Tracie was right there in front of Mary Lee every day, letting her undeveloped potential shine. She was the reason Mary Lee pushed herself so hard to learn all she could about the art and science of coaching gymnastics –

about drills and progressions and spotting. Tracie's raw potential and Mary Lee's own sense of duty, her own sense of obligation, drove the new coach to improve in every way she could.

Tracie was the reason the doggie boxes had to be cut into the ceiling and roof. It was clear that if she progressed, she'd soon be whacking her body against the ceiling or slamming full force into a wall. Tracie was the reason they opened the closet up and had the girls start their vault sprint from in there. Tracie was the reason for excavating the floor and putting the foam pits in.

And Tracie was the reason Mary Lee hit the road and asked other coaches to teach her all they could about various maneuvers, about sequences and skill progressions, and about spotting athletes as they learned skills that were inherently dangerous. Mary Lee went at the task of becoming a good coach the way she went at everything: with humility and a straightforward passion for excellence.

She called the coach at Losantiville and got his agreement to help her learn all he could teach her about Jaeger and Hindorf release moves on bars. These were skills that Mary Lee believed Tracie could learn, but they were dangerous and demanding, and Mary Lee wanted to know them inside and out before having Tracie try to learn them.

"Hi. I'm Mary Lee Tracy," she said to the coach who met her near the bars in the Losantiville Gym. "I'm here to learn everything you can teach me about those two skills. I've read all I could find about them, and I've watched every piece of film I could get my hands on. I want to know it all – what the judges look for, how you teach athletes to do the skills, how you break the move down and how you progress the athletes through the sequence, and most importantly, how you spot these skills. I'm all ears." After Losantiville, she visited GymOhio, and then others. She even left the city and visited gyms in Columbus, Indianapolis, and Michigan, and often flew to visit other gyms in more distant cities, where good coaches agreed to help her learn. Mary Lee Tracy absorbed everything she could.

Day by day, event by event, skill by skill, Tracie, the athlete, and Mary Lee, the coach, improved. Nothing happened overnight. There was no magic moment, no "suddenly everything came together" point in time. Getting better was hard work, and it took time. But they worked hard, and they grew.

Five years later, in 1989, after the doggie boxes and foam pits had been built, and by practicing her vault sprints by launching herself out of CGA's storage closet, Tracie Halstead made it to USA Gymnastics' National competition, representing Region V. With the help of her ever-improving coach, Tracie had become one of the top fifty American gymnasts in her age group. She also earned a full scholarship to Ohio State for gymnastics.

It was Tracie who was behind Mary Lee's remarkable growth. It was for Tracie that Mary Lee pushed herself so hard. It was for Tracie that she kept on learning and improving. It was Tracie who helped her become a pretty darned good coach. It was Tracie who helped push Mary Lee to become the coach she was capable of becoming, to be recognized and honored as USA Gymnastics' Region V's Coach of the Year. Tracie was her muse.

And Tracie got her ready for Amanda.

Inside CGA, note bathroom behind the human pyramid.

Closet door (vaulters launched their sprints from inside) and doggie box.

CHAPTER 18

AMANDA

Lynne Ruhl fingered through the girls' tops that hung on the rack in Arlan's Department Store in the Cincinnati suburb of Finney-town. It was September, 1989, and school had just started. Becky, now fourteen, was sprouting taller and needed a few new tops. Lynne wondered whether she should select tunics or pullovers. She couldn't decide.

"Well, hi there, Lynne," a voice said from across the clothing rack. Lynne shook off her absorption with tops and immediately recognized Patty Borden, her long time friend, who now stood right next to her.

"Oh hi, Patty!" Lynne said with a friendly smile. "I'm sorry. I was so focused on my shopping I had no idea you were right there."

"Getting a top for Becky?" Patty asked.

"Yes, "said Lynne. "If I could ever make up my mind about what to get her. I suppose the bigger challenge is finding something she'd actually wear." Both women laughed aloud, sharing the bond of moms who hunt for clothes that must pass the fashion-focused scrutiny of youngsters.

"How is Doug?" asked Lynne. "And what's the latest with Bryan and Amanda?" Doug was Patty's husband, and both were old high school friends with Lynne. Bryan, their son, was a few years older than their daughter, Amanda. Lynne's daughter Becky competed at times against Amanda, who was also an avid gymnast. Becky almost always got better scores than Amanda, though Lynne, the ever observant gymnastics judge, knew that Amanda had phenomenal potential.

The two old friends chatted easily and shared all their latest. They got caught up on families and schools, on which kids had which teachers this year, and on recent summer activities.

One part of Lynne's brain was in the conversation. The other part secretly wrestled with whether she should say anything about Amanda's gymnastics. Lynne had seen Amanda perform for a few years now, and she believed Amanda had tremendous potential. Sure, Lynne's own daughter Becky beat Amanda in scores, but that was because Becky was coached by Mary Lee, who Lynne knew was one of the best. Becky was talented, but she had no business outscoring Amanda, Lynne thought to herself. But if Amanda were ever to join up with Mary Lee… And yet the fraternity of gymnastics parents had its unwritten rules, and one parent would do well to not suggest such changes to another. It wasn't polite. It wasn't proper. And it really wasn't any of Lynne's business.

And yet, didn't she owe it to her true friend to speak the straight truth? Lynne, the judge, saw things other gymnastics parents hadn't been trained to see. Lynne, the judge, saw Amanda's remarkable talent and knew that Mary Lee could make the most of it. And she knew that if Amanda stayed put, her potential was not likely to ever be fully realized. Should she say it? Would it hurt Patty's feelings? Was it altogether inappropriate? She so wanted to say it, to just blurt it out.

"So like I was saying, Amanda's got Mrs. Milo this year," said Patty, "and I have mixed feelings about that, you know. Plus all her time in the gym is going to make it tougher than ever. Amanda works so hard in the gym, but she's not winning many events, and that's really demoralizing after a while, you know? You're a judge, Lynne, and, well, I've been wanting to ask sometime what you thought about all that. And Bryan, well – "

"Patty, listen to me," Lynne interrupted, responding with instinct as much as with deliberate choice. She leaned in and locked eyes conspiratorially with her dear friend. She had started, and now there was no going back. Lynne took a deep breath and then spotlighted truth. "Patty, your daughter has more potential than any kid I've seen. She needs a great coach to help her, and she needs it right now. Do not wait. Do not pass Go. Do not collect two hundred dollars. Do not delay. Get your daughter registered at CGA *now* and get her signed up with Mary Lee. Your daughter has what it takes to make the Olympics, Patty – do it now."

The words were all out before Lynne could check herself, before she could filter and choose words carefully. She had blurted. And though it was the truth, it probably violated some part of the Gymnastics Parent Code. Lynne felt a bit out of line, and embarrassed, stated abruptly that she had forgotten something and needed to go, and she headed for Arlan's door.

A week later Amanda Borden was training under Mary Lee Tracy at CGA. In the interim Patty Borden had done her homework. She had checked out CGA; some of the gym's athletes had been qualifying to compete at Regionals and Nationals over the past few years. And Patty had checked out Mary Lee, who had pushed herself for Tracie, who had helped Tracie earn a spot on the First Team at Nationals in '86.

Mary Lee's reputation was growing, and Mary Lee was now ready for Amanda.

(L to R) Lynne Ruhl,
CGA gymnasts Karin Lichey and Amanda Borden,
and Mary Lee Tracy

CHAPTER 19

UPWARD

All the hard work from 1983 onward had begun to pay off in gradual increments. Increasing numbers of CGA athletes were placing higher in competitions and earning spots at prestigious events. The place was earning credibility the old fashioned way: they were earning it.

Success and winning can be contagious things, and CGA was becoming that kind of place. They were making it happen by maintaining their focus on core values, on respect and trust, and on the idea that everybody they encountered deserved to be treated with basic human dignity. There were no magic bullets, no "secrets" to their success. The culture had been built, and it continued to sustain and strengthen itself. And it formed the foundation on which the bricks of hard work and relentless pursuit of excellence were laid.

Good performances inspired better performances. Hard working athletes inspired one another. And the trend of steadily improving scores attracted talented athletes.

Mary Lee again received Region V Coach of the Year honors in 1990. CGA athletes were winning college scholarships – one in '87; one in '88; three in '89 (including Tracie Halstead's full ride at Ohio State); and two more in '90.

Staying the course was a particularly tough thing to do once successes began to roll in. Those first big wins and accomplishments whet the appetite for more victories and tempted the CGA leaders and staff to press for more. Those successes gave a ready excuse for diminishing the focus on culture and dignity, for easing away from things like Bible Study and teamwork and "niceness," and for going hard after even more wins. But Lynne and Mary Lee resisted. They stayed the course. They pursued more wins, to be sure, but not at the expense of their stated goals and values. And in so doing, CGA positioned itself for true greatness.

It would all come at them sooner than they thought. The 1992 Olympics were just around the corner, and coming fast.

CGA was succeeding
by maintaining their focus on core values,
on respect and trust, and on the idea that
everybody deserved to be treated with
basic human dignity.

CHAPTER 20

AMANDA - 1992 ASCENT

The peak age for women gymnasts is 15.7. Amanda Borden would be 15.2 when the 1992 Olympic torch would be lit, and the opening ceremonies would take place in Barcelona. She'd be almost exactly in her physical prime as a gymnast, at her absolute statistical peak as an athlete. The timing could not have been much better.

Yet she knew the Olympics were a long shot. She had the potential; she knew that. So did the CGA staffers. But lots of athletes had the physical potential to make it. At the elite competitive level she was entering, the critical differentiator between one athlete and the next wasn't always physical. Very often it was mental. It frequently got down to things like attitude, confidence, and good old mental toughness: blocking out distractions and pain, and overcoming missteps and adversity. That and experience. Relative to others, Amanda was short on experience, very short. She was aware of all those things. She was realistic. She had her head screwed on remarkably well for a fifteen year old. Amanda Borden kept things in perspective and remained aware that making the Olympic team was unlikely. Still, it was the Olympics, and like every athlete, she dreamed her dreams.

But first she'd have to compete at Nationals,[4] and do well enough there to earn an invitation to compete at the U.S. Olympic Trials in Baltimore. If she performed well enough to make it to Baltimore, she could then compete for a spot on the U.S. Olympic Team. Those were no small hurdles. America's best would be giving it their all, and many of them had been on this stage before. The truth is that some were Amanda's heroes. They were athletes she had looked up to. She had sought their autographs and had posters of some of them hanging on her bedroom wall. Now she'd have to compete against them. And she'd have to beat at least some of them to have a shot at the Olympics.

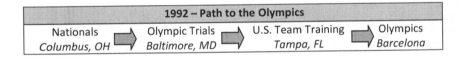

In May of '92, just a couple of days after her fifteenth birthday, Amanda was sent forth from CGA amidst cheers and well wishes, surrounded by enthusiastic supporters brandishing banners and holding signs proclaiming their unconditional faith in her. She headed to Columbus, Ohio, and the Ohio State campus, the site of the U.S. National meet. The CGA family was proud of her. Making it to Nationals is a momentous accomplishment and honor for any competitive gymnast. And Amanda's invitation to compete at Nationals reflected well on all of CGA. They wanted her to do her best.

---

[4] Over the years the U.S. National Championships have gone by different names, sometimes called "Nationals" and sometimes called "USA Championships," etc. For the sake of consistency and to make this simpler for the reader, I use "Nationals" throughout.

Yet the harsh truth is that most did not think she would perform well enough to make the cut for the Olympic Trials that would follow Nationals. This was a whole other level, an entirely different thing. They expected Amanda would do her best in Columbus, that she'd represent CGA in a way they'd all be proud of. They expected she'd gain some valuable experience that she could later draw on during future competitions.

They also knew that she was hurting. Gymnasts almost always have some ailments, because their bodies take such constant poundings. Jarring landings and falls during practice take their toll. Not only does gravity yank them down from remarkable, soaring heights, but gymnasts twist and torque and spin their bodies all the way through their descent and into their landing. It's rough on them. It's rough on joints and ligaments; it breaks bones; it tears muscles. A year earlier, Amanda had broken a growth plate in her left elbow, and then tore her right hamstring soon after. Then in January, just a few months before Nationals, doctors discovered that she had contracted a disease in her elbows, and her bones were not growing correctly. That forced her to take several weeks off from gymnastics, and that had made her timing a bit rusty. During all this she did her best to stay in shape and maintain her timing, flashing around the gym in a cast, moving as best as she could, rehearsing her routines mentally, though not physically.

Three days later she returned from Columbus. The CGA family practically threw a ticker tape parade for their returning hero. She had done it! She performed wonderfully, beyond expectations, really, and finishing fifth, qualified for Olympic Trials. Nobody from CGA had ever qualified for Olympic Trials before. They celebrated Amanda's remarkable success – and their own. They could scarcely believe it.

There was quite a buzz over the next few days. Press releases, interviews, and people from all over offering their congratulations and asking about the nuts and bolts of competitive gymnastics. They were trying to put it all in context. A kid from their home town, a regular, down to earth, hard working Midwestern kid from Cincinnati was going to get a rare shot at making the U.S. Olympic Team. And Amanda was perfectly cast for the part: perky, bright, energetic, humble, clear-minded, with an irresistible, winning smile (her nickname was Pepsodent), and a last name that conjured up milky wholesomeness. Amanda Borden gave them something to be proud of. In early June she'd be off to the Olympic Trials in Baltimore.

Only twelve were invited to compete. The top seven from that meet would make the U.S. Olympic Team, though there was some confusion about that criterion. The U.S. Coach, Bela Karolyi, had stated that the top eight gymnasts from Baltimore, plus Betty Okino, who had won silver at the previous year's world championships and was recovering from an injury, would make the team and train for the Olympics in Tampa. The U.S. Gymnastics Federation said it would be the top seven from Baltimore, plus Okino. Either way, the goal was to finish in the top seven.

Hardly anyone thought she had a realistic chance of succeeding in Baltimore, but that wasn't the point. She had been invited! She had *already* succeeded, just by getting into the fray. She'd been invited to compete with the likes of Shannon Miller, Kerri Strug, Kim Zmeskal, Dominque Dawes, and other stars. (For those uninitiated in the sport: these names constituted gymnastics' version of Mickey Mantle, Roger Marris, and Willie Mays. Only Mary Lou Retton stood larger, she being the Babe Ruth of the bunch, now twenty four and too old to make her body compete at this level.) Amanda would be on the floor with them, competing directly with America's best, and because of that, she had already succeeded.

She trained hard, and June came. The CGA Family was ecstatic about one of their own making it to the Olympic Trials. Amanda felt ready, despite the normal aches and pains every gymnast constantly deals with. But she earned a poor score on her very first event in the competition, the vault. Her push-off from the vault table wasn't quite right and consequently her balance was off during her flight, and that caused her to not stick the landing. She earned a 9.337, a remarkable feat for mere mortals, but not good enough for an Olympic hopeful. It was the lowest of all vault scores. Poor Amanda...

She bounced back and put the fluke behind her, exercised that special mental toughness that overcomes profound adversity. She performed well for the rest of the meet. Two days later, when the dust settled and the scores were tallied, Amanda Borden, who trained on vault by sprinting out of a closet and soaring under "doggie boxes" cut into CGA's ceiling, who worked around the bathroom that was smack In the middle of CGA's floor, finished seventh all-around. Seventh... She had made the 1992 U.S. Olympic Team!

Inside CGA, doggie box over vault

CHAPTER 21

AMANDA – HOLLOWED OUT

The mood around CGA was downright giddy – and surreal. Amanda had succeeded beyond their wildest expectations and even beyond what many dared to hope for. It was just so hard to believe. It took a while to sink in. Every time people at CGA tried to piece it together in their minds, they lost their breath and, finding it so hard to grasp, had to start all over. There was a sort of delightful cloud over the place, a dreamy and delirious mist of success so marvelous and wonderful, yet so unfamiliar and unexpected, as to give the place a fantasyland feel. Perhaps only Amanda and Mary Lee remained grounded and focused. They had the Olympic Games just a month away and coming straight at them; they had to prepare.

The controversy started right away, but didn't get resolved until a couple of weeks had passed. Would the top seven from the Olympic Trials really make the U.S. Team? The top eight? And how would the scored rankings actually be decided? Would they include only those gymnasts who actually competed in Baltimore, or would others who didn't compete there be scored as if they had competed at the trials?

Two gymnasts who did not compete in Baltimore petitioned the U.S. Gymnastics Federation and asked to be included on the team.

Betty Okino had suffered a stress fracture in three vertebrae, which prevented her from competing at Nationals in Columbus and at the Olympic trials in Baltimore. Michelle Campi did compete at Nationals and finished third, but injured herself right before the Olympic Trials. Both had trained under Bela Karolyi, who had been named the 1992 U.S. Olympic Coach.

After some wrangling and much politicking, it was finally decided. Campi and Okino, despite their injuries, were in. The remaining top six from Baltimore were in.

Amanda Borden was out.

They took it from her. What she earned on the floor, during competition, they took from her. It wasn't that Okino and Campi weren't good. Of course they were. But they didn't earn it on the floor. Yet they were chosen and Borden was "un-invited." Wendy Bruce, who finished right in front of Amanda at Baltimore, made it. Amanda's score was 77.248. Wendy earned a 77.381. Wendy made the team, went to Barcelona, competed, and stood on the Olympic podium to receive her bronze medal. Amanda watched on TV from home. 0.133 was all that separated her from that podium, less than two tenths of one percent. She had come so close....

CHAPTER 22

RESILIENCE

It rocked her. She was just a high school kid. She was a solid student. Amanda Borden, the bubbly kid with the short, bouncy, blonde hair and world class smile, the kid who had taken flute lessons and who would be homecoming queen, the kid who would graduate summa cum laude from college, felt like she had her heart ripped out.

She'd had it. She was done.

She was tired, drained. Exhausted. Demoralized. She went to school like other fifteen year olds, and then went home instead of going to the gym, as she had done for years. Dealing with it, accepting it was hard, and her head spun in disbelief. At fifteen and on a near-global stage, the world thrust on her what ultimately thrusts on all of us as adults: the cold reality of unfairness, which ruthlessly crushes our idealistic view of the world. Amanda sleep-walked through the next few weeks of her life. She cried the hot tears of letting-go, the tears of injustice that accompany us when we begin to accept that our best efforts were just not enough, and that we will never grasp the thing we so long ached for. When we begin to accept that the thing was never ours to hold, and it never will be.

But deep habits are deep habits, and they stay put in our deep-down places. They operate outside the realm of logic or emotion, and they pull on us and propel us without regard for judges, scores, or gut-wrenching news. Amanda's deep habits eventually carried her back to the gym, not to work out and compete, but to just be there. She would drift in and sit on a bench and just watch. Nobody knew what to say to her.

Lynne Ruhl eased up next to her on her second day back and just sat there. She was simply present, nothing more. After a while Amanda began to talk, and Lynne made it her job to listen. They found privacy in the gym's modest "office," a box of a room jammed with papers and files and two chairs along a wide shelf that served as a desk. Amanda talked. She talked a lot. It was that kind of talking people do when they don't know what they need to talk about, but they get everything out of themselves and spread it on the table in front of a friend, in hopes that something good might emerge. Lynne just listened and stayed attuned for anything that would give insight about how to be helpful. Lynne listened as Amanda shared her exhaustion and her decision to walk away from gymnastics forever. Lynne just wanted to be supportive and to help Amanda make the right decision, whatever that turned out to be, as long as it was clear-minded and based in reality.

Several talk-filled days later, Lynne finally heard it. She heard the words from Amanda that became insight for Lynne.

"And besides," said Amanda as she ran over her verbal inventory of reasons to stop competing. "I'm fifteen now, and the next Olympics is four years from now… Nineteen is too old to be an Olympic gymnast…"

"Say that again, Amanda."

"I said that I'm fifteen now, and I'll be nineteen when the next Olympics happens."

"And…?"

"And nineteen is too old to be in the Olympics – at least as a gymnast."

Lynne's intent listening had finally uncovered the nugget of gold that allowed her to be helpful. She knew that Amanda's assumption was faulty. She knew that nineteen was not too old. Unusual, yes, but not at all out of the question. Amanda was operating from an assumption that simply wasn't true, and Lynne knew that she could best help Amanda by helping her stay grounded in truth.

Lynne asked, "Is that really true, Amanda? Is it true that nineteen is just too old?"

Amanda said, "Well, yeah, of course it is."

Lynne asked, "Would you do something for me, Amanda?"

"I guess so. Sure."

"Would you please go home tonight and research that? Go research it and see if nineteen really is too old for the Olympics."

The next day, Amanda came back to the gym and came straight to Lynne's office. She wasn't smiling that Amanda Borden Smile, but the despair she had been carrying in her eyes was gone.

"Oh, my gosh," said Amanda. "You were right; I couldn't believe it."

"What did you find?" Lynne asked.

Amanda pulled the list from her pocket and began to list the names she had researched the previous night.

"I went back to Helsinki in '52," she said. "I'll start with the gold medalists first. Maria, thirty-one years old. Larisa won gold twice, once when she was twenty-two and again at twenty-six. Vera won twice also, at twenty-two years old and at twenty-six." She interrupted herself and looked up at Lynne. "Now things were different in those years, you know," Amanda said.

"I know. Keep reading."

Amanda continued. "Ludmilla, twenty. Nadia, fifteen. Yelena, nineteen. Mary Lou, sixteen. Yelena, the other Yelena, nineteen..."

Amanda continued through her list, naming the silver and then bronze medalists along with their ages.

There was a long silence when she finished. Then Lynne asked the question that carried an inescapable answer. "So, is nineteen really too old to compete as an Olympic gymnast?"

Amanda's eye contact was steady and firm, though still not enthusiastic. "No," she said plainly, flatly. "No."

"I agree," said Lynne. "Now, understand that doesn't mean *your* body can take that much training and punishment. It doesn't mean you wouldn't have to do all over again every bit as much work as you have already done, and more. And it doesn't mean that even if you did, you would necessarily be good enough four years from now to be at that level. And it doesn't mean that even if your body *can* take it, and even if you *do* work that hard, and even if you *are* that good, that the exact same thing won't happen to you again. If you continue, there would be a chance that you could do all those things and still not make it to the Olympics."

Amanda was taking it all in, noncommittal, but listening.

Lynne continued. "So the question for you, Amanda, is this. Knowing all that, but also knowing that being nineteen is not an automatic disqualifier, do you still want to continue? Or, on the other hand, and knowing all that, is it time for you to stop? Nobody but you can decide. I just want to make sure you make your decision on facts, honey, and not on any assumptions that are faulty."

"Thanks," was all Amanda could muster. It was sincere. She was still exhausted. She was still demoralized. But now she had a little different perspective. She had something to think about. Thinking about it would help.

She thought. She prayed. She listened – to her mind, to her body, to her soul.

Slowly, gradually, over a period of weeks, Amanda Borden made her way back into leotards, and Cincinnati Gymnastics Academy. She migrated from talker, to active watcher, to casual workouts, and finally to intensely competitive workouts. She never announced anything formally; there was no press release. But Amanda was back. Armed with the sober awareness of the world's unfairness and having zero guarantees, she had decided to stick with it after all.

What a difference that decision would make.

It would change her life. It would change Lynne's life and Mary Lee's. It would change the lives of others. And eventually, it would even change mine.

PART FOUR

GOLD

CHAPTER 23

JAYCIE – AT THE BOTTOM

Watching Amanda Borden from afar was thirteen year old Jaycie Phelps. The Junior Elite gymnast from Scottsdale, Arizona, didn't think she was on track to ever get to that stage herself, but she loved seeing the American women do so well at the Olympics. She so very much looked up to them.

Jaycie followed the lead up to the 1992 Olympics, the selection of the U.S. Olympic Team, the political maneuvering and petitioning of the U.S. Gymnastics Federation, and the un-inviting of Amanda Borden from the Olympic Team.

Jaycie was glued to the television for the Olympics themselves, and watched with pride as the U.S. women's gymnastics team took third. She was mesmerized as they stepped up on the podium and were benighted with those precious bronze medals. It all seemed so magical. It seemed so distant.

The "Unified Team," that is Russia, the old Soviet Union, took the gold, as they had in every women's gymnastics Olympics competition since 1952. The only Olympics since '52 they didn't win was the one they boycotted. That was in 1984, when the Berlin Wall still stood strong and The Cold War hung like a storm cloud over the world. Romania won gold that year. Romania was the other world power in gymnastics, finishing second, behind Russia, in each of the last five Olympics.

The U.S. had never won gold in women's gymnastics. Not ever. Of the forty-two team Olympic medals awarded since gymnastics became an Olympic sport in 1928, only two had gone to the U.S (one bronze and one silver), and one of those was in the year the Russians boycotted. Jaycie watched on TV in 1992 as American women earned another bronze. That brought the U.S.'s grand total of Olympic medals in women's gymnastics to three, two bonze and one silver. The Russians now had ten, all gold.

	Team Olympic Gold Women's Gymnastics
1952	Soviet Union
1956	Soviet Union
1960	Soviet Union
1964	Soviet Union
1968	Soviet Union
1972	Soviet Union
1976	Soviet Union
1980	Soviet Union
1984	Romania*
1988	Soviet Union
1992	Soviet Union ("Unified Team")

The USSR's gold medal dominance in Olympic women's gymnastics
was even stronger than it was in ice hockey.
(*The USSR boycotted the 1984 Olympics in Los Angeles)

Jaycie had dreamed those big, Olympic-sized dreams once. There was a time, a couple of years earlier, when she thought she had a shot to make it to the top. But that dream was slowly slipping away, and it saddened her. As hopes and aspirations incessantly leaked out of her, they seemed to take a part of her with it, and Jaycie felt the ache and inner emptiness that accompanies lost dreams.

She had started gymnastics in her home town, a small place in

Indiana, and rose up fast in the sport. She was pretty good as an eleven year old, when she realized she had probably developed as far as her modest hometown gym could take her. That's when she and her family had a serious discussion about her talent and dreams, and decided, as many competitive gymnastics families do, to pull up stakes and move. The Phelps family moved to Scottsdale, Arizona. There was a world class gym there, and Jaycie's parents were willing to put the rest of their lives on hold, to patch together whatever they could around career and living arrangements so that their daughter could pursue something they knew was burning deep inside her.

So the Phelpses moved to Scottsdale and Jaycie gave gymnastics all she had to give. But month by month, she could sense it wasn't going to be enough. For some reason she could never quite pinpoint, it just wasn't working as she had hoped. She was progressing. She was nationally ranked, and that, at least, was something to be proud of. Jaycie was in Junior Elites, the highest level of gymnasts in the age group too young for Olympic qualification. But she knew she wasn't at the top of that group.

One way or the other, Jaycie felt she needed to make a decision. Either she was going to move forward and achieve bigger things in the sport, or she needed to accept that her best days were already behind her. One way or the other, she told herself, she had to decide. Her parents had transplanted themselves for her, and she was deeply appreciative of their sacrifice. But she couldn't ask them to continue sacrificing if she had achieved all she was capable of. With every passing meet, with every passing month, her confidence shrunk and another piece of her earlier dream drifted further away. She was growing tired. But she was determined to give it one last shot with whatever she had left.

Jaycie earned an invitation to the Junior Nationals competition in Orlando in March of 1993. She would compete against the twenty-five best American gymnasts in her age group, Juniors, and the results would tell her precisely where things stood. Despite her doubts, she trained hard in preparation, and she and her parents left for Orlando hopeful if not confident.

The morning of the event, Jaycie felt more of a sense of doom than excitement. Her stomach's butterflies weren't the ones that fluttered and tickled and made her anxious for the bright lights and the chance to succeed. Her butterflies were instead those oversized, heavy, lethargic ones that just sat there, wings barely moving, nearly lifeless. She and her parents were remarkably close, and so she knew they'd understand.

"Don't come today," she asked softly, eyes down, as she was leaving them for the competition.

"But honey, we came all this way and we're so proud of you. This is Nationals!"

"I know, I know. But I just know I'm not going to do well, and I don't want you to have to see that. I don't want to disappoint you... and honestly, I don't want the pressure of knowing you're watching – I just know I won't have a good day out there."

Jaycie met her parents' eyes and held them with her own. Her pleading eyes said it all again, wordlessly. She looked down again because she couldn't take those eyes straight on.

"Please," she implored one last time. "Don't come."

And thirteen year old Jaycie closed the hotel room door behind her and headed toward the gym and competition, like a failed gladiator marching to her execution.

Several hours later, inside the buzzing building, athletes performed their warm-ups while loudspeakers blared out names and hometowns. Excitement filled the air. Jaycie did her best to get mentally prepared though a part of her was just going through the motions.

At the same time, Jaycie's father slinked in the hallway shadows and stayed well out of view. He didn't want her to see him. But he had to be there. Even if she failed, even if she had her worst day ever, he loved his daughter dearly and was intensely proud of her.

Truth be told, it had little to do with gymnastics. But he was proud of her gymnastics too, regardless of how today might go. When Jaycie's name was called for each event, her father crept forward into the little pedestrian tunnel that opened up into the gymnasium, stayed in the shadows, prayed, and watched.

Jaycie Phelps finished twenty-fourth out of twenty-five at that meet. She was right; it didn't go well. Her parents were profoundly proud of her anyway.

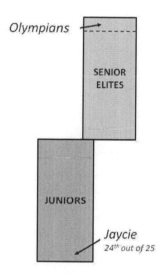

"So I think that's it," she said to her parents as they arrived back home in Scottsdale. "I had a good run," she added, trying to adopt the best attitude she could. Talking about it in past tense, saying "had" instead of "have" or "having" intrigued her. It suggested all was over and done with, yet that sentiment didn't square with her completely. A part of her had indeed given up. A very real part of her was deflated and defeated. And yet, when she said the words out loud, something small but nevertheless alive in her objected, shook its tiny fist and seemed to mouth silently but insistently, "Not yet!"

Her parents both reacted calmly, as if they knew this conversation was coming. "Why not take some time and let things settle a bit before deciding anything," said Jaycie's mother. "It might be best to sleep on it for a few days," added her father.

Jaycie spent the next few weeks trying to figure things out. She talked it through with her parents, and then talked it through again. They wanted what was best for her, but it was hard to know what that was. They told her it didn't have to be about winning and achieving; that the simple love of the sport was still a good thing, a great thing, and that might be enough. They prayed together. They thought. They waited.

A month later, with the help of loving parents, Jaycie came to her decision. She'd give it one more try. One more shot. But she wanted to go home, and so did her folks. They missed their little town in Indiana; they missed relatives, and roots and Midwestern ways. On top of that, Jaycie needed a fresh start, needed to be where she had a chance to work through all the junk in her head, all the disappointments, all the lack of confidence, all the sense of defeat and despair. She needed a place where she could heal....

That kid in Cincinnati, that Amada Borden, the one who almost made it to the Olympics and her own bronze, she trained at a gym up there. If they were good enough to get Amanda to the Olympic Trials – and almost onto the Olympic Team – well, they were good enough for Jaycie. It wasn't exactly in her home town, but it was only ninety minutes away, and the Phelps family decided they'd find a way to make it work. Jaycie would give it one more shot. And she'd do it at CGA.

CHAPTER 24

JAYCIE – HEALING

"I always make an extra effort to focus and 'read' a new athlete when I first meet her," Mary Lee Tracy would later tell me. "I could tell right away that Jaycie had low confidence and low self esteem. She was quiet and withdrawn. She couldn't look me in the eye."

So things at CGA started slowly for Jaycie. In those early days, Mary Lee mostly just observed. She talked with Jaycie and listened carefully. She was patient. She really didn't know what Jaycie was capable of, but she knew the only way to find out was to first help her regain her confidence. She was a good athlete and a good gymnast, but Jaycie seemed to be the only one in the gym not aware of that fact.

It was tough on Jaycie. Her confidence was badly shaken. She was trying to learn the ways of a new gym. Because her family returned to their hometown and to old jobs that were ninety minutes away, Jaycie had been put up with a CGA family in Cincinnati. They were wonderful people, generous and embracing, and they practically adopted her. They welcomed her with full hearts. But still it wasn't the same as truly living at "Home." They were family, but they couldn't be "Family." She was also trying to get familiar with a new school and make new friends. And she was doing all this to pursue a dream that might be dead and gone anyway.

"Mostly," Jaycie said, looking back on her earliest experiences with Mary Lee, "she listened. She talked with me and listened. But she

115

did more than that, I think. She listened with more than her ears. She listened with her eyes as she watched me perform my routines. She watched my body language during breaks. Her listening went way beyond just hearing the words I said. I felt listened to. I felt respected. And over time, I began to trust her. And eventually I got to where I trusted her completely. That made all the difference."

Mary Lee didn't care about the athlete. That could come later. First, she had to care about the person. Once she found the person, once the person got healed, the athlete could emerge. Nobody really knew what kind of

> "Our chief want is someone who will inspire us to be what we know we could be."
>
> *Ralph Waldo Emerson*

potential Jaycie Phelps actually had. Mary Lee was true to the CGA philosophy; the place was not about producing great athletes. It was about producing great people. And that's exactly how Mary Lee approached Jaycie: by caring for the person and helping her to become the best person she could be.

Like many parts of this story, Jaycie's return to competitive gymnastics, her return to her winning ways, her return of confidence, her return to *herself*, didn't happen suddenly. Changes came slowly, gradually. Yet they came with an unmistakable certainty.

Jaycie was bouncing back. Jaycie had begun, once again, to believe in Jaycie. And she bought into the system, bought into her coach, bought into the CGA Way. The culture at CGA was quite different than what she experienced elsewhere, and it took her a while to trust that it was all real. Listening classes. Bible Study. Social gatherings. Mutual support. Trust – real trust amongst the entire CGA community. Bit by bit, Jaycie tested it out, dipped her toe in the water of CGA, and allowed her vulnerability to show. Over time, she came to see it was all quite real, and Jaycie eventually opened up in ways she hadn't done for years. As Jaycie the Person got better, Jaycie the

Athlete began to emerge.

With the help of Mary Lee, Jaycie had found something – some drive, talent and potential – that she never before knew was in her. She was soaring. She had gone from not really knowing all the reasons she was performing badly, to not really knowing all the reasons she was excelling. Maybe it was as simple as having somebody caring enough to listen, patient enough to let Jaycie be Jaycie, and skilled enough to help her improve. Maybe it was as simple as being surrounded by a culture that embraced human dignity and respect.

In twelve months, Jaycie Phelps went from twenty-fourth in Juniors to sixth in Seniors. She was more than "back." She was, in fact, finally on her way.

She was healed.

Jaycie on beam at CGA

Mary Lee Tracy receiving coaching accolades

CHAPTER 25

OLYMPIC HOPEFULS '96

At Cincinnati Gymnastics Academy, things progressed as they always had, with a commitment to constant improvement and a focus on the person first and gymnast second. Athletes improved and earned increasingly impressive scores, and that translated into invitations to events of greater stature. And all that, in turn, attracted more talent to CGA. Their ranks swelled, and they literally outgrew their humble gym. Mary Lee, running what had now become a financially sound and growing business, bought a new facility and moved CGA there. No more doggie boxes. No more bathroom in the middle of the floor. No more vault runs out of a storage closet. No more annual bug infestations. CGA had arrived.

Teamwork permeated everything they did. One might think that Amanda and Jaycie might have developed a certain rivalry, given that only seven could ultimately be chosen for the U.S. Olympic Team. But that never happened. Pushing each other happened. Stretching each other happened. But it wasn't out of competitive fear; it was from mutual support, encouragement, and example. The CGA culture had taken root inside them. They cared about each other, rooted for each other, hoped for and prayed for the best for each other. Before the competition began at each meet, the two would find a moment together, pull out their Bibles, and pray. They'd pray for competitors and families and judges and for everyone's safety. They'd pray for friends and families in need. And they'd pray for God's grace, that they might perform at their best, that people might see their joy, and that they could accept whatever happened that day. They'd thank their Maker for their gifts of gymnastic talent. They'd always finish with Philippians 4:13, the passage painted big on CGA's wall: "I can do everything through Him who gives me strength." It was more than an individual sport to them. They were all about team.

Meanwhile, Mary Lee Tracy's unique approach hadn't gone unnoticed, nor had her successes. USA Gymnastics named her Region V Coach of the Year in '89, '90, 92, '93, and '94. She was also named USA Gymnastics Women's Coach of the Year in '94 and '95. In '92 and '94, CGA was represented at World Championships and Pan Am Games. Amanda and Jaycie were fully on the big stage. So was Mary Lee.

1996 – Path to the Olympics			
Nationals *Knoxville, TN*	Olympic Trials *Boston, MA*	U.S. Team Training *Greensboro, NC*	Olympics *Atlanta, GA*

For Amanda, 1995 was a particularly tough year. She had been on a tear, placing among the top five on the U.S. National Team in '93, '94, and '95, and earning silver at the '94 World Championships in Germany. She had fully bounced back from her disappointment in '92 and had been pushing her body past its statistical gymnastics prime, all in hopes that her body would stand up to the pounding punishment, and that her exacting precision and balance wouldn't begin to slip away. After three years of that, and just one year before her goal of the '96 Olympics, she suffered a broken hand and then a broken toe. She knew those would heal in time for the Olympics, but she also knew her body was feeling the strain, and the months off from training were going to hurt her. Deeply driven, and encouraged by her CGA Family, she nevertheless pushed on. She had to be ready when the qualifying meets were held in June of 1996.

In the meantime, Jaycie had recovered from a knee injury and surgery, and she was delivering strong, consistent performances. With her confidence back and solidified, she earned spots on the U.S. National Team and won medals in World Championships competitions in '94 in Germany and '95 in Japan. She just kept getting better.

So Mary Lee would take Amanda and Jaycie to Nationals in early June in Knoxville. They finished third and fourth, respectively, clearly qualifying them for U.S. Olympic Trials a few weeks later in Boston. Throughout both events, the two CGA gymnasts hugged and cheered each other and offered selfless encouragement to others. And gymnastics aficionados in attendance watched a coach who broke the mold by treating her athletes as people rather than as property. It was clear that she demanded their best, but it was also clear that she respected them. It was a novel approach that ran against the grain of conventional wisdom, and there were plenty of skeptics.

In Boston's Fleet Center, Amanda and Jaycie finished side by side once again, placing fourth and fifth in Olympic Trials competition. Mary Lee beamed and hugged them both in irrepressible joy. Dreams were coming true.

Then, in a surprise move, USA Gymnastics named Marta Karolyi (Bela's wife) as the U.S. Women's Olympic Gymnastics Head Coach and Mary Lee Tracy as Assistant Coach. It would be the first all-woman coaching staff in forty years. Up to that point, nearly everyone had assumed the coach would be Bela Karolyi, famed defector from Eastern Europe and hard-line gymnastics coach known for his intimidating coaching style – and for winning at all costs but winning nevertheless. Bela had coached Nadia Comaneci and Mary Lou Retton, and he had been the U.S. Olympic women's gymnastics coach in the last two Olympics.

Yet USA Gymnastics had seen something in Marta and in Mary Lee, who had placed two gymnasts on the team, which seemed to promise more. The Olympic team would have different coaches and a different coaching style than in recent years. It would later prove to be a momentous decision.

America's newly named 1996 Olympic team met and congratulated each other in a small locker room under the bleachers in Boston's Fleet Center. They would soon be known as The Magnificent Seven: Amanda Borden, Jaycie Phelps, Dominique Dawes, Shannon Miller, Amy Chow, Dominique Moceanu, and Kerri Strug. They put on their red, white and blue and walked out onto the floor, as *Proud to be an American* blared out over the loud speakers, and 17,000 fans roared their pride and approval. It was their first act as Team.

Amanda, now healed emotionally, Jaycie, now healed in confidence, and Mary Lee, the humble coach who put character development in front of winning, were headed to the Olympic Games.

CHAPTER 26

"TEAM"AND OLYMPIC GOLD

Training camp for the Olympic team was held in Greensboro, North Carolina. Though it only lasted about a week, it was a critical part of their story. Here, more than at any time in recent history, the U.S. Women's gymnastics team became Team. Here, they worked and trained and ate and socialized together. Here, they did *everything* together, both on the floor and off. Here, they bonded. Here, directed by their coaches, they agreed that team gold, not individual scores, would be the goal.

When two of the team members, plus the hands-on Assistant Coach, all bring the same culture to a group of seven, it spreads. A positive, supportive, respectful, winning culture is a powerful thing, and it is irresistibly attractive. It is contagious because its virtues are self-evident, and because it resonates within all of us. When we see it, when we witness it, we immediately want it; we won't go without it.

By unanimous vote, the ever-smiling Amanda Borden, the most positive, vivacious, encouraging, supportive teammate any athlete could ask for, was named team captain. The very same Amanda who, through culture and caring and hard work, overcame crushing injustice and now exemplified positivity. And it was decided that the team's first competitor, the lead-off gymnast who would take on that tremendous pressure and set the tone for them all, would be Jaycie Phelps. The very same Jaycie who, a few years earlier, could not make eye contact with her coach.

They were soon in Atlanta, the site of the biggest Olympic Games in history (to that point). Three billion of the world's people watched the spectacular opening of the Twenty-Sixth Olympiad. President Clinton kicked off the opening ceremonies on July 19th in the brand new Centennial Olympic Stadium. Mohammed Ali lit the Olympic torch. It was magical…

Two days later, on July 21st, wearing their country's colors and led by their team captain, the U.S. women's gymnastics team marched in unison onto the floor of the Georgia Dome. Thirty-two thousand thrilled voices erupted and shook the walls of the place. Amanda Borden looked up in confidence, smiled her beaming smile, and waved. The team followed suit; the crowd roared even louder; the love affair had begun.

> A positive, supportive, respectful, winning culture is a powerful thing, and it is irresistibly attractive. It is contagious because its virtues are self-evident, and because it resonates within all of us. When we see it, when we witness it, we immediately want it.

Jaycie and Amanda, as they always did, found each other before the first event, held hands, and prayed their prayer, Philippians 4:13, "I can do all things through Him who gives me strength…" Then Jaycie led them into battle and set the standard, made them proud. Bars, beam, floor, vault; that first day was compulsories. They did well. As the day came to a close, the U.S. was behind the Russians, the Unified Team, but ahead of Romania, both of whom were odds-on favorites to finish #1 and #2 respectively.

On the 23rd they competed in the "optionals" part of the competition; it would be the final day of the Olympic gymnastics team events. Just as before, the crowd went wild as the U.S. Team entered. Just as before, they prayed and supported each other. Just as before, their captain led them out and Jaycie bore the burden of being the first U.S. competitor. They had a chance to catch the Russians, but Romania was right on their tail. Scores went back and forth as the day unfolded, and the tension mounted as things came down to the last few events.

The crowd, fully aware that the underdog U.S. team was close to a historic upset win over perennial powerhouses Russia and Romania, was electrified. The air was charged. They chanted, "U-S-A! U-S-A!" They waved flags and pumped their fists in the air in support. They hushed as American gymnasts began their routines and exploded in delight when they finished. The Georgia Dome could barely contain their hope and excitement.

Hardly anyone knew it at the time, but they already had enough points to win – even though Dominique Moceanu fell on both of her vaults, in the last event of the day. Dominique's miscues had suddenly taken the wind out of their sails, and what seemed like a solid U.S. victory and a gold medal was in jeopardy. But they had the option to scratch Dominque's score and use Kerri Strug's. Kerri would be the last U.S. gymnast to compete; the vault was one of her best events. She would vault twice; the best score would be used. Meanwhile, Russian gymnasts were nailing it on the floor exercise, piling up points and pouring it on strong. The U.S. and Russia had been neck-and-neck all day.

Perhaps you already know how this ended. Perhaps you already know that Kerri inexplicably missed the landing on her first vault and fell, badly injuring her ankle. Perhaps you already know that America, watching from millions of living rooms across our country, gasped in our national disbelief and felt that hopes for Olympic gold would again slip from our collective fingers. Maybe you were one. Perhaps you already know that despite her pain and injury, despite literally not being able to feel her leg, Kerri Strug, fully aware that she was injured and should step down, said a prayer, and lined up a second time. She started her final run almost eighty feet away from the vault table, forced her strained body to perfectly hit her mark at forty-five feet, and then delivered a vault that lives colossal in the history of sport and courage. Keri Strug stuck her landing, hobbled on one foot, and assured U.S. Team gold.

What you probably don't know is that Kerri Strug went into the Olympics experience with the primary objective of individual medals. What you probably don't know is that not only did Kerri sacrifice her body for "team," she sacrificed her decades-long dream for a team that had formed just two weeks prior. She let go of the thing that drove her for all those years; let go of the fire that burned in her and dragged her out of bed so early all those mornings; let go of the thing that pushed her to bounce back after all those injuries, that drove her to relocate away from her family and endure coaches' criticisms that had at times brought her to tears. She sacrificed that thing, that ten year long dream and passion – for team. Kerri Strug sacrificed a lot more than her body.

Such is the power of "team."

Such is the power of culture.

She knew that in making that second vault, in forcing a second landing on that already damaged ankle, she would not be able to compete in subsequent individual events. But she did it anyway, and she did it heroically. Her momentous vault deserves its place in history as a pinnacle of athletic courage, of triumph of willpower over pain. And it should also be known as one of history's greatest triumphs of team over individual, of culture over self. Kerri, who went into all this with her own personal goals, surrounded by the irresistible power of respect and encouragement, sacrificed everything for team.

The other thing you probably don't know is that for the first time ever, the global television broadcasting network of the Olympics, in this case NBC, put a microphone on Mary Lee Tracy, the coach who would interact most with the athletes on the floor. During the unfolding drama, NBC brought sight and sound from Mary Lee and her athletes to the world. And for the first time ever, the world of gymnastics saw and heard a coach interacting with her athletes in a way that had previously been almost unknown in the sport. They witnessed a coach who listened as well as directed. They saw a coach who expected the best while still showing profound respect. They heard a coach care deeply for her athletes, for the *person* that was in that leotard. And they saw her win.

Led again by their selfless captain, the U.S. Team took the tallest podium. Thirty-two thousand thundered with uncontrolled exuberance in the Georgia Dome. They knew that they had seen something great, that they had just witnessed history. *The Star Spangled Banner* was played while a huge U.S. flag was raised higher than the rest. Millions more across the U.S. and around the globe, eyes wet with the tears of inspiration, hearts pounding with pride, watched as gold medals were hung on each team member of the 1996 women's Olympic gymnastics team. It was a glorious moment for the United States of America. It was a glorious moment for sports. They had upset the Romanians. And they had done the unthinkable: they had upset the perennial, global favorites, the Russians.

> In Olympic gymnastics, the Head Coach must manage a myriad of issues, not the least of which is dealing with the press and coordinating with the International Olympic Committee. She is, of course, most concerned with her athletes... but the distractions and pressures force her to be somewhat externally focused. She has but little choice.
>
> By contrast, the Assistant Coach is there to work directly with the athletes on a day-in, day-out basis. She pulls mats and adjusts equipment, and is highly focused on her athletes. It is therefore the assistant coach that is closest to the gymnasts.

Lynne Ruhl watched from the stands, where she sat next to the Borden and Phelps families. She took it all in through tears of amazement and pride. And in her way of quiet Midwestern humility, she thanked God for the gifts that surrounded her.

Mary Lee wasn't the head coach, and Jaycie and Amanda weren't the stars; they weren't the big names. Neither Jaycie nor

Amanda qualified for the individual events that would follow over the next few days. Their scores weren't high enough; they weren't good enough.

Those three from CGA? All they did was lead by example, form TEAM, assistant-coach it and captain it and serve as lead-off gymnast... and help bring home the *first ever* women's Olympic gymnastics team gold in American history.

Jaycie Phelps and Amanda Borden, Olympic Gold Medalists

CHAPTER 27

PROMISES KEPT

The next few weeks were a blur. Reporters, cameras, and requests for appearances were overwhelming. Somebody wanted them on the *Today* show, and a call came from the White House. Television cameras and reporters were everywhere. The flurry of autograph sessions and interviews were dizzying. Cameras flashed wherever they went; fans yelled words of joy at them; nameless faces stuck microphones in front of them and asked every conceivable question. Letters, cards and telegrams came in from around the world. Agents and representatives appeared from *CNN*, the *Tonight Show*, *Letterman*, and every newspaper and magazine imaginable. There were endless sponsorship and spokesperson deals, and *Wheaties* wanted them on the front of their cereal boxes.

Soon after the Olympics, the team was whisked around the country to perform exhibition events in local gymnasiums, packed with adoring, pride-filled, inspired crowds. Thirty-one cities in fifty-nine days. The chance to see their Olympic winners up close was a thrilling prospect for Americans, who came out in droves to meet and cheer them. America couldn't get enough of them. It was tough on the team, as they went from town to town, hotel to hotel, interview to interview. As soon as one exhibition ended, they headed off to the next one. They performed in local coliseums and in high school gyms, in civic centers and on college campuses. They were thrilled to do it, but they were running on fumes, on a sort of adrenaline high. They loved it, but going through it felt trance-like.

Back at Cincinnati Gymnastics Academy, classes and local meets went on as always. Every eye and every heart had been affixed to the Olympics in Atlanta, of course, but operationally speaking, it was business as usual. Coaches coached. Gymnasts trained and competed. A few gymnasts bid farewells to their CGA family because parents were relocating for jobs, etc. New athletes called to inquire about joining CGA, and many of them did join. Lynne Ruhl greeted the newcomers and helped them ease into the CGA system and organization. And she continued to conduct her classes, as always. "We're all about respect and dignity…" she always began.

Reporters called CGA constantly, of course. "When are they going to be back in Cincinnati?" And, "can you call us as soon as you know, so we can be there with cameras when they step off the plane?" Could Amanda make this event and could Jaycie make that one? Could Mary Lee speak at this group's annual meeting in two weeks? It was as if the whole city had won a gold medal. Reporters from other countries wanted to schedule appointments to film stories about Mary Lee, CGA, and their two Olympians.

It had all happened so fast – Nationals and Olympic Trials, training as a team in Greensboro, Team Olympics and Individual competitions. It had been a whirlwind. Their remarkable success was hard to grasp, hard to process and digest. Yet it tasted as sweet as anything could, and Mary Lee relished every moment, trying to wrap her mind around all that had happened, all they had done together.

It was late October, and the team was near the end of their

exhibition tour. It was less than three months after the Olympics, and the magical dust of excitement and sudden celebrity had not yet settled. Mary Lee, trancelike with gratitude and wonder, drifted away from the floor where her team's exhibition program had just ended. They had signed countless autographs and the athletes were now in the locker room, getting ready to get in the bus and go the next city on their tour.

Olympic Gold Medalists: Jaycie, Mary Lee, and Amanda

Mary Lee just needed to move a bit, to walk, to think. She meandered, absorbed in her thoughts, and rolled it all over in her mind. At last she found herself in a quiet corner, tucked under some bleachers, alone. She sat down on the floor and closed her eyes, thanked her God for this still impossible to comprehend experience, and opened her Bible. As she did, a piece of paper that she had not looked at in years fell from its pages, fluttered for a moment, and landed in her lap. It was yellowed from the years, tattered and falling apart at its creases, feathered on its corners. She opened it and read what had been written thirteen years earlier, when the idea of buying a gym still sounded ridiculous and risky and absurd:

> 1. *One day Cincinnati Gymnastics Academy will be nationally and internationally known.*
>
> 2. *One day Cincinnati Gymnastics Academy will change the way gymnastics is being trained worldwide.*
>
> 3. *One day gymnasts from around the country will be moving to Cincinnati to train. They will be thinking they are coming for good gymnastics, but we are to know they are coming here to heal.*

Tears flooded her eyes and her skin tightened. She took out her cell phone and dialed the person that had given her that piece of paper, her old friend back at CGA, Lynne Ruhl. Lynne was still in her office at CGA when the call came in.

"Hello, this is Lynne."

"Oh, Lynne...it's Mary Lee." She was reeling, and it was hard for Mary Lee to get anything out. She felt dumbstruck and could only choke words out haltingly. "Lynne... it's all coming true."

Lynne just listened.

"It's happening," Mary Lee said. "What you wrote, what God had you write in 1983; it's happening. The first one says, 'there will come a day when Cincinnati Gymnastics Academy is nationally and internationally known." The emotional Mary Lee could barely get the words out.

"Mary Lee," Lynne said. "Take a deep breath, my friend. You only know the half of it."

"What do you mean?" said Mary Lee.

"The phone hasn't stopped ringing here," said Lynne.

"Coaches and Olympic committees from several countries want to come visit CGA to study how we're doing things, how you're treating the athletes so differently than the other coaches are."

"Oh, my gosh," said Mary Lee, blushing under the bleachers, alone.

"That's not all, Mary Lee," said Lynne.

"What is it?" Mary Lee braced herself for what Lynne would say next, though she couldn't imagine anything coming at her that could possibly bigger than what had come at her over the last few months.

Lynne took a deep breath. "Mary Lee," she said, "they're coming. Those kids, those athletes who need gymnastics coaching and need to heal. They're coming..." Lynne rattled off name after name of America's most competitive gymnasts, the highest level gymnasts and future Olympic hopefuls, whom in recent weeks had called CGA and said that they wanted to train there.

There was a long silence between the two of them. They both, in their own ways, were struggling to comprehend all that was happening – all that *had* happened. They both recalled that crazy conversation, thirteen years earlier, when Lynne leaned in toward Mary Lee and stated with such certainty that *it was already done...*

Within three months of the end of the 1996 Olympics, thirteen of the U.S.'s fifty training elites had already moved to Cincinnati and joined CGA. Coaches and committees from around the world were coming to learn from CGA, and they would revamp their entire approach to coaching gymnastics. And young athletes were coming to CGA for better gymnastics... yet Lynne and Mary Lee knew they were really coming to be healed.

Those three impossible promises – they were all coming true.

"There are three stages in the work of God: impossible, difficult, done."

James Hudson Taylor
19th Century Christian Missionary

CHAPTER 28

"THE HOSPITAL"

They flooded the place over the next several months. They were everywhere. There were reporters, filmmakers, directors, and producers making documentaries. Coaches and national Olympic committee members came to learn a new way of coaching gymnastics. Aspiring athletes and their families were constantly visiting. The onslaught was almost impossible to deal with, and in the face of such an enormous wave of popularity, Lynne and Mary Lee did the only thing they could do: stay focused on their priorities. They continued to do what they said they'd do, to match their actions to their words, to stick to the same philosophies that had taken them all the way to the top. They cared more about the person than they did about the gymnast. They remained more concerned with what kind of women they were producing than what kinds of scores their gymnasts were achieving.

Competitive gymnasts left places where coaching was done in the old mold, in the Eastern European model of harsh, aggressive, forceful, and demanding ways. Some of the kids had been broken. Many had been damaged. But they didn't seem to know it, to even be aware of it. They were attracted to CGA because of good gymnastics, good fundamentals, good basics, clean lines in performances and gold medals at the end of the rainbow. They didn't even know that the thing they needed most was simply to be healed. They weren't aware that they could never achieve their gymnastics goals if they didn't first heal. *The Chocolate Milk Story,* as it later became known, illustrates just how damaged some of the athletes were and how healing enabled subsequent breakthroughs in performance.

Elite, competitive athletes in need of healing had been arriving in droves. Lynne and Mary Lee noticed right away that something was wrong with each of the damaged young athletes, but they struggled to identify just what it was. Whatever it was, it wasn't healthy; it wasn't desirable; it wasn't natural. Those athletes didn't interact and mingle like the CGA athletes did. They didn't even seem to have personalities. Whatever their problem was, it wasn't good.

Mary Lee and Lynne decided that until they could figure out just what "it" was that was wrong, they would keep those newcomers isolated. They would quarantine them. They didn't want "it" infecting the culture they had worked so hard to build and which was producing such phenomenal results.

One day, Lynne's daughter Becky, who had been a CGA gymnast and who was now pursuing a degree in psychology, suggested a simple exercise that she hoped would expose the underlying issue. She had learned about the test in her class, and she hoped it might be relevant at CGA. The next day, Lynne did the experiment that Becky had suggested.

Lynne called the troubled athletes into a large room at CGA. She then placed on the table in front of each athlete a small glass of white milk and small glass of chocolate milk. She instructed each of them to taste from each glass.

"Taste some white milk. Taste some chocolate milk." She gave them a few seconds to complete the simple task.

"Have you each tasted both the white milk and the chocolate milk that is in front of you?" she asked each of the ten athletes.

"Yes," each answered.

"Which one do you prefer?"

It was as if she had asked for the logic proof for the Pythagorean Theorem. They were stymied. Dumbfounded. They simply stared at her, blank faced, while she repeated the question.

"Which one do you prefer, white milk or chocolate milk?"

"I don't know," was the most comprehensive answer she could manage to extract. It was almost like they didn't comprehend the question. They were literally incapable of answering.

Their awkwardness and discomfort grew, and a few of the athletes actually began to get emotional and tear up. Lynne didn't let them off the hook; she insisted on hearing their answers. One of the girls, Liz, eventually became so frustrated with the incessant, unanswerable question that she burst into full blown tears, ran out of the room, and charged Mary Lee on the gym floor, demanding to know which she (Liz) preferred.

"Mary Lee! Mary Lee, which do I like, white milk or chocolate milk? Lynne is *making* us answer!"

It finally became clear. These athletes had been so conditioned by previous coaches and supervisors to do as they were told, that they literally did not even know their own preferences. In the most literal sense, they had been "trained," but they had not been "coached."

So Mary Lee, Lynne, and the CGA staff set about the business of coaching instead of training. They listened. They challenged. They helped athletes see themselves as they really were, helped them remove the false ideas and beliefs they held about themselves. They helped them take responsibility for their own successes and failures. They found the person that was inside the athlete, and they drew that person out and drew out the greatness that was already there. The critical work wasn't on the gym floor. The critical work took place in private conversations and later in group sessions. The critical work started with respect for self and respect for others, and then with each athlete's gradual assimilation of the CGA Way. The important work on the gym floor came much later.

Wounded athletes arrived with shattered egos. Some arrived with gaping holes where their confidence used to reside. Some brought with them their fears and insecurities and self doubts. Some brought their anger. Some brought their distorted, sometimes convoluted ideas about what they could achieve and what they deserved from life, about the source of their gifts and the purpose behind their talents. They came, and they indeed were healed. So much of it happened in those first several months and so many athletes began to significantly improve their national rankings after training at CGA, that USA Gymnastics began referring to the place as "The Hospital." The nickname didn't emerge just because athlete's scores got better, though they were literally transformed. It emerged because it was obvious to everyone (except the athletes) that at CGA they were being healed and liberated in a way that made it possible for them to achieve more.

Those were heady days, top of the world days that were warmed by the glorious glow of recent Olympic medals. CGA had become "the place" in the world competitive gymnastics. CGA appeared to be a place of alchemy, seemingly able to convert any and all raw materials into gold – literally.

It would have been easy for "Team CGA" to assume the mantle of celebrity and greatness. They had earned it. They were stars, whether they wanted to be or not. Nobody would have blamed them if they had migrated toward more and more elite coaching, toward spending time exclusively with only the best of the best. Yet, led by Lynne and Mary Lee, they remained rock solid. Despite all the new demands on her, Mary Lee still made time to be directly involved with *all* her athletes, regardless of talent. To this day, some of those CGA athletes who were "less than world class" are touched by memories of a selfless Mary Lee, by a world class coach who invested in them when she could easily have left them to the attention of "lesser coaches." Instead, she led by example. She lived by the statement of purpose CGA adopted so many years ago. She lived by it when it would have been easy not to.

At *The Hospital*, every patient mattered. At *The Hospital*, healing was for everyone who needed it.

CHAPTER 29

RESULTS
THAT MATTER

When your goal is to produce good people, when you claim to care more about the person than the gymnast, then you should probably measure your success not by medals but by life's more human standards. There's nothing wrong with medals and ribbons and first-place placards. But do they really matter?

Amanda Borden is married and is a proud mom. She also is an employer and coach. Amanda owns Gold Medal Gymnastics, a two-facility operation near Phoenix. I watched her on the floor with her kids, coaching and training them. It was obvious: she cared about the person first, and the gymnast second. Her goal? "My goal is to touch the lives of children all across Arizona to help them reach their goals, whatever they may be." She still smiles endlessly. She coaches the coaches. "Believe" is written in enormous letters on the gym wall.

Still skeptical, wondering if maybe I just caught the young coach in a rare moment of perfection, I asked one of the moms as I watched the afternoon unfold at Amanda's gym. "I'll bet she's got a tough side, a mean side we're not seeing right now," I suggested, inviting secret criticism.

The mom standing next to me looked at me like I was out of my mind. "I think she can be tough," the mom said. "But never mean. These kids *love* her. They'd do *anything* for her... And so would the parents. I couldn't ask for a better influence in their lives."

"I thought so," I said. "I was just egging you on to see if maybe I was missing something," I confessed.

"You're not missing anything," she said. "Amanda Borden is the real deal."

And so she is. Thank goodness somebody spent time with her and listened to her – and *cared* for her – when she was so close to walking away from this sport in 1992. That changed Amanda's life. And in turn, through Amanda, it is still changing lives.

And, oh yeah... her gym is the home of State, Regional and National Champions. And the place doesn't even have doggie boxes.

Jaycie Phelps recently opened a top notch competitive gym in her old hometown, near Indianapolis. The Jaycie Phelps Athletic Center (JPAC) hosts gymnastics, softball and baseball. She opened it to give back to the small town where she grew up, to give the place the kind of gym that wasn't there when she was a kid. That's the kind of person she has become: hard working and selfless. A job creator. A person whose place is all about "helping the youth of the community create a way of life that will fulfill the future of each individual through health, happiness and personal growth." She works hard at treating everyone she encounters – regardless of the gymnastics talent, or whether they are athletes, parents, employees or vendors – with respect. Thank goodness Mary Lee earned her trust, back in those days when Jaycie was ready to quit and couldn't even make eye contact.

"Enter with a Dream," is painted over the door when you walk into JPAC. Indeed.

And, oh, in case you are wondering... even though she's only had the doors open for eighteen months, JPAC just had a Junior Elite qualify for USA Nationals. JPAC is already on its way.

Cincinnati Gymnastics Academy and Mary Lee Tracy continue in their tradition of dignity and respect – and winning. Their stated vision: *"At Cincinnati Gymnastics we are determined to provide every child, regardless of their ability, with high quality gymnastics instruction. Their relationship with us will help them develop character and gain confidence as well as gymnastics skills. The success of Cincinnati Gymnastics will be measured by this growth in the children whose lives we touch."* And still prominent: *"I can do all things through Christ who strengthens me. Phil. 4:13."*

I recently visited CGA and on the way out, I grabbed a few current flyers from the front desk. They were for parents and athletes, and I wanted to see what kinds of things were being communicated within the CGA community. I half expected to see a list of competitive meets, individual scores, exercises for beginners, and things like that. But no. The fliers were about active

> Treating people with respect and dignity did not conflict with achieving greatness. In fact, just the opposite proved to be true: it enabled greatness.

listening, teaching kids to share, and the health benefits of laughter. Go figure.

Mary Lee and her gym have gone on to produce multiple world champions, National Team members, and Olympians. CGA is regarded by all as one of the most elite gyms in the world.

Becky Ruhl, the subject of that 1983 phone call that started this whole story, never competed at the Olympic level. She trained at CGA for years, and she became an outstanding gymnast. But her decade of dedication to CGA gymnastics never brought her to the national or international podium, never brought her to a grand Olympic stage. Instead it helped her with something bigger.

Several years after she retired from gymnastics, Becky was diagnosed with a rare disease. Ehlers-Danlos syndrome is an inherited disorder marked by defects in the connective tissue, and that in turn adversely affects joints, muscles, ligaments, blood vessels, and visceral organs. She has had it her whole life, yet for the first thirty years nobody knew. Strangely, it made her more flexible than the average person, which no doubt helped her in gymnastics. At the same time it made any given gymnastics maneuver tougher for her, and it probably contributed to her many injuries. For eight full years Becky was essentially bedridden, and on three separate occasions she came close to dying; the doctors didn't think she would make it. But Becky Ruhl is a fighter. She's tenacious. She's tough as nails. And one day at a time, she's making it.

There is no cure for Ehlers-Danlos, but at long last her symptoms are generally under control. Becky recently earned her degree as an RN, and she wants to practice nursing for adult trauma and ICU work. She earned straight A's. She's got a profound depth of compassion for others who are suffering. She has a lifetime of understanding adversity and pain. And she's cool under pressure, clear-thinking and decisive. People are attracted to her. They like being around her. She's committed to helping others, to serving them. Becky Ruhl never became a world class athlete. She became a world class person.

The list of names goes on, and now, through CGA's web of graduates and those touched by what CGA leaders built, their legacy extends in ways we can probably never know. They are still today touching others in a thousand unseen ways.

Treating people with respect and dignity did not conflict with achieving greatness. In fact, just the opposite proved to be true: it enabled greatness. The CGA Way produces much more than great gymnasts. It produces great people.

And that's what *really* matters.

PART FIVE

LESSONS

CHAPTER 30

CULTURE DRIVES RESULTS

The lessons and principles from this story seem to sit plainly in front of us, self-evident and confirmed. The overarching message and core concept is one that resonates in our hearts and makes sense in our places of intuition and instinct. Yet it still chafes a bit. It's as if we came out of the womb taking the notion for granted, accepting it as true, and then gradually, through decades of schooling and "conventional wisdom," we have learned to un-believe it, to deny it. This story, this bit of history tells us to again believe, to re-embrace what has always made sense in our deepest places, where our Maker inked it in crimson on our hearts.

Culture drives results. The way we interact with people significantly impacts their performance and their contributions to the bottom line. Valuing people is not only the right thing to do; it is the proven path to the best in human performance. Culture is not an afterthought, a nice-to-have, a feel-good thing that we can worry about after we get the bottom line results we need. It is the very thing that enables great results, and it is the very thing that, when it's wrong, gets in the way of the outcomes we want. When it comes to organizational performance, culture is not the cherry on top of our ice cream sundae. It's the bowl the whole thing sits in.

CGA didn't start with great coaches and top-notch managers. There was no first rate facility when our story began. CGA wasn't studded with amazing athletic talent in the early days. But by focusing on culture first, those very same raw ingredients literally produced world-class, global-game-changing results. When Lynne received those three impossible promises, God didn't reach into our midst and perform "magic." It wasn't God that made those things happen; *people* did it. I believe God promised those outcomes to Lynne and Mary Lee because they were already committed to the principle of putting people first.

The story forces us to question why God would make such promises to such unlikely people in such unlikely circumstances. Did He want to prove to Lynne and Mary Lee that He could work wonders, that He could perform "magic" by producing unthinkable outcomes from the lowliest beginnings? Did He feel a need to show us He's that powerful? Maybe "God" had nothing to do with any of this, and those promises were something Lynne simply invented one morning in 1983. Maybe she simply divined the future via some special skill of premonition. Maybe it's all just a big coincidence.

These attempts at explanation make no sense to me.

The only thing that does make sense is that God wanted us all to know that Lynne and Mary Lee had the formula right: *Focus on people first. Treat everyone with profound respect and dignity. Pursue excellence and have high expectations but never let those things cause us to mistreat people, to take advantage of people, to treat them as anything less than remarkable.*

The only thing that makes sense is that God wanted us to know that when leaders get the culture right, human performance soars. Those three impossible promises were not just for Lynne and Mary Lee. They were for all of us.

* * * * * * *

What follows is a high level discussion of culture. The following chapters are designed to put culture in proper perspective and to define the fundamental keys to building a great culture. They are not intended to be a comprehensive text, but rather to give you a correct framework and help you start the culture building process.

CHAPTER 31

TRUTHS
ABOUT PEOPLE
AND LEADERS

This story also challenges our deepest beliefs about people in general and about the role of leaders. It suggests three fundamental truths that are perhaps even more provocative than the idea that culture drives results. These ideas can run counter to what we may have heard and what we may have been taught. They may even directly conflict with what we think we have learned through our own experiences. These ideas will no doubt be met with scorn and ridicule by some, and some will dismiss the ideas as sophomoric and naive. At the very least, for most of us, our heads will have trouble accepting these three ideas.

But as before, they also harmonize with our instincts, with our gut intuition, and with the story we have just experienced. Our hearts, it seems, already know these things are true. Our hearts find them positively undeniable.

Taken together, these truths collectively hold the power to literally transform any organization:

1. **People (*all* people) are created with remarkable talent and amazing potential – beyond what most of us can even imagine.**

This seems a rather overstated proposition – that all people inherently have enormous talent and potential. Haven't we all encountered people who, to put it politely, seem to suggest otherwise? Yet, if this message were not true, the story we just read could not have happened. It did. Who in their right mind would have indentified the original cast of characters in the CGA's story as a sure bet team to achieve gold medal results? They did. And it happened because that talent was already in those people, that potential was already there. We're probably all familiar with the little chestnut, "God made us, and He doesn't make junk." Consider the possibility that maybe that's actually true... Indeed, every one of us has greatness already in us – literal, world class greatness that was put into us when we were first formed.

> "Our deepest fear is not that we are inadequate.
> Our deepest fear is that we are powerful beyond measure...
> We ask ourselves, 'Who am I to be brilliant, gorgeous, talented, fabulous?' Actually, who are you not to be? You are a child of God...We are all meant to shine, as children do. We were born to make manifest the glory of God that is within us.
> It's not just in some of us; it's in everyone..."
>
> *Marianne Williamson, Author*
> *A Return to Love*

This is not to say that anyone can do anything. Not all of us can be Olympians. Not all of us can even be great clerks or great sales reps. We're not all cut out to be world class CFO's or top notch warehouse assistants. But we're all capable of more. We're all capable of achieving more than most bosses think we can – and we're capable of doing more than even *we* think we can. Real greatness is indeed in all of us.

2. **The core job and obligation of the leader is to draw that talent out and unleash it. Leaders don't need to fix people or manipulate them. Their job, indeed their duty, is to refine the gold that is already there.**

Once we accept #1 above, this premise follows rather naturally. If you, as a leader, are surrounded by literal greatness; if you don't have to pump greatness into them, then it follows that your job is to pull that greatness out. The greatness and talent may not be evident at first. Indeed it rarely is. Yet how different any workplace or organization might be if the leader operated from a conviction that greatness is already there.

What about revenues and profits? Shouldn't the business organization's leader be focused on revenues and profits? No. (Keep reading; I haven't lost my mind.) Revenues and profits are the deliverables *of the organization*; that is why the organization *exists*. Let the organization do what it is there to do, which is to deliver revenue and profits.

The leader, on the other hand, is there to enable the organization to do what it does. The leader is there to get the best out of the people in it.

If the leader draws out the greatness from the people in the organization, they'll deliver revenue and profits beyond anything that could be imagined.

"The task of leadership is not to put greatness into people, but to elicit it, for the greatness is there already."

John Buchan
Scottish author and Governor General of Canada

---

3. **The best way to draw out the greatness that's already in people is by managing culture. Conventional wisdom considers this a "soft skill," and the implication is that it is therefore a "less than" skill, residing among the second tier of leadership skills. Yet it is the single most significant thing any leader can do.**

If the raw potential is already in the people, and the job of leaders is to draw the greatness out, then how should leaders do that? Should they cajole? Encourage? Cheerlead? Leaders do it best by managing the one thing that nobody else can manage: culture. Leaders intentionally create the culture. Leaders manage it. Leaders care for it. It is the single most important thing any leader can do.

> "It can be argued that the only thing of real importance that leaders do is to create and manage culture."
>
> *Edgar Schein*
> *Award winning author and professor*
> *MIT Sloan School of Management*

Before a leader can effectively create and manage culture, that leader must first understand what culture is – and what it isn't.

CHAPTER 32

ACCURATELY UNDERSTANDING CULTURE

The main reason why culture has yet to be universally embraced and fully leveraged as a key business driver is that we have failed to accurately understand what "culture" really is.

Much of the conventional wisdom from recent decades has made culture synonymous with things like values, standards, operating principles, organizational artifacts, heroes, and a group's storied legends. Much of the well-intentioned thinking has been that if we get clear on these things, inscribe them on the plaque in the conference room, talk about them at our annual meetings, and celebrate them in our corporate lobbies, then we will have managed culture. Some say culture is about pizza parties and dress codes, about flexible work hours and company outings. Some will use catch phrases like, "work hard, play hard," and "compete to win."

Others tell us to go deeper. They say that culture is in how we do our business – how we position ourselves in our industry, how we compensate people and make decisions around things like promotions and advancements. They say it is about how we provide benefits like health care and education reimbursement.

These are all good things. There's nothing wrong with

studying them and improving them. There's nothing wrong with fretting about how to do them in the best ways possible. But they are not what drives culture, nor are they themselves "culture."

Properly understood, culture is the water in which all these things swim. It is, at its most core and fundamental level, how 1:1 human interactions are conducted in an organization; and that, in turn, reflects what is believed about people.

To really get at culture, we have to get at what leaders in an organization fundamentally believe about people, and how people in that organization interact with one another. "Culture" rests in things like whether we respect one another, whether true listening occurs, whether we build trust by consistently matching actions and words, whether we dispel untruths, and whether we confront one another in healthy, constructive ways. It rests in whether we truly believe that literal greatness resides within all people. It rests in whether we truly treat everyone with profound respect and dignity. It rests in whether leaders believe all people deserve respect because of their humanity, or whether they think respect is something that has to be earned.

How we as leaders do (or don't do) these things will be reflected in our work processes, our people systems, and in our decision making and leadership norms. It will show up in how we position our business and in how we design and manage our work systems. It will show up not in whether we do golf outings (which doesn't matter), but if we do such an outing, it will show up in how we behave toward others leading up to and during the golf outing (which does matter). It will show up in how we handle problems and in how we act when living up to our stated core values actually costs us something. It is rooted in what leaders fundamentally believe about people.

All these things will produce whatever business results they produce, and in the process, they will reveal our real norms, our real heroes, our real values. That's because those things are not drivers of culture; they are outputs *from* culture.

152

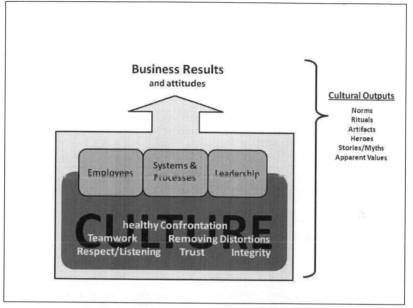

Organizational Culture & Performance Model
Culture is at the core; it is the water in which everything else swims.
It is in how people interact at a 1:1 level on a daily basis.

Culture is about the quality of individual, 1:1 interactions that occur thousands of times every day in an organization. Culture is about how we treat one another, and it's about what we believe to be true about people and organizations. Those interactions will color all of our business practices, our business decisions, and the daily conduct of our work. All these things, in turn, will ultimately impact our business results and organizational outputs.

Now that we have a framework for accurately understanding culture, how can a leader go about creating and managing culture? How does one "do" culture?

"It is only with the heart that one can see rightly; what is essential is invisible to the eye."

Antoine DeSaint-Exupery

CHAPTER 33

HOW TO BUILD CULTURE

Culture building demands a methodical, systematic approach. Though it deals with those messy, organic, sometimes fluid and unpredictable things called people, the deliberate creation of culture nevertheless lends itself to a straightforward, proven model. This model provides a roadmap for leaders, and it yields predictable results.

A common problem is that we want to start at the end of the culture building process. We see the manifestation of conflict and inappropriate confrontation; we see the damage these things do in our organizations. We see disengaged employees and unhealthy office politics. And we naturally want to address those problems, believing that if we do, then the great culture we want is just around the corner. We are tempted to think that if we could just get rid of this person or change that one, things would instantly and permanently get better. We are lured into thinking that if people would just adopt a better attitude, if they would just choose to be more positive or would just stop fighting leadership at every turn, then things would get better. Then our culture would finally improve.

But people and cultures don't work that way, and it is important that we don't get distracted addressing symptoms rather than dealing with fundamental causes.

Culture-building model – four steps for how to build culture

This systemic model guides us in methodically building cultures which will produce strong, sustained results. To do that reliably, we must follow a four-step approach, which I describe here only at a very high level.

First, establish an environment of profound respect, which is best done – and can perhaps only be done – by consistently practicing effective listening skills. This may sound deceptively simple; it is not. Effective listening (like all the skills inherent in applying this model) is a learned skill. It is not innate, and this plain fact is often an enormous stumbling block for leaders. It is not easy to do, and it does not come to us naturally. We have to learn how to do it, and must apply the skill deliberately before it will become second nature.

Second, build trust by spending time together and, most importantly, by doing what we say we'll do. The only way to truly establish trust is by matching words and actions, even – and especially – when it hurts. And then we have to practice this consistently over time. The cliché is so very true: Our actions speak louder than our words. This simple formula defines what it takes to build trust:

$$\frac{\text{INTEGRITY + SKILLS + COURAGE}}{\text{Applied Consistently over TIME}} = \text{TRUST}$$

Behaving with integrity comes at a cost. Living up to our word means that sometimes we'll lose a client. Sometimes it means we'll even lose money. Sometimes it might mean we'll have to apologize. But when people in an organization finally come to believe that the leader's words and principles mean more than circumstances do, then that leader will have established something truly powerful beyond belief: *Trust*. And that's contagious. When people in the organization trust the leader, trust spreads and multiplies itself. Trust at the top begets trust throughout; trust grows exponentially. People in the organization change, and organizational trust becomes something they start to own.

Third, remove distortions by first identifying them and then by helping others who hold such distortions to discover truths for themselves. We can only do this after respect and trust are solidly in place, and we do it best when we stay firmly rooted in caring for the other person, no matter what. Efforts to remove distortions can only work when they come from a place of genuine, selfless caring. This is what Lynne did for Amanda when she asked Amanda to research whether nineteen was truly too old for her to compete at an Olympic level. It wasn't about getting the answer Lynne wanted. It was about helping Amanda discover the truth for herself.

Fourth, challenge and confront one another in healthy, constructive ways. This is about calling out the best in each other. It is about commitment to our goals and to our words. Once the first three pieces of the model are in place, we do this step by simply pointing out the discrepancy we hear or see in others – how their actions don't match their words. We do it best when we do it factually and unemotionally, when we do it without judgment, and when we hold ourselves accountable for our own integrity.

Truths about the Culture-Building Model

- Each of the culture-building steps requires learned skills. They are not innate, and we do not naturally know how to do these things well – though it is tempting to believe that we can. Such seductions are like sirens of the sea, calling us toward hidden rocks that are certain to sink us. Seemingly subtle changes in our approach can make the world of difference. Get some help. Learn and acquire the skills, especially listening and trust-building. It will prove to be one of the best investments you can make.

- Culture-building can only be done in-sequence. You must first establish respect (Step 1) before you can make any meaningful progress on building trust (Step 2), and so forth. That's not a reflection of you or your ability to do more than one thing at a time. It is a reflection of human nature: People won't allow you to establish trust with them until they believe you respect them. ("If I don't believe you respect me, I will *never* be able to fully trust you.") You cannot skip a step nor do these steps in parallel. The universe and human nature will not allow it. Stick to the sequence and you'll be rewarded.

- As you move through the process, you'll find that each step becomes exponentially easier to do, because the critical enabling step(s) before it has been completed. If you don't first have a solid environment of respect, if you haven't yet clearly established trust, good luck trying to help someone change their distorted view of the world. And even better luck to you as you try to confront and challenge that person. On the other hand, once respect is in place, once we trust one another, once we've removed our distortions and misunderstandings, confronting one another in healthy and constructive ways is actually a piece of cake. It really is.

- As a consequence of all this, you should expect that building culture will take time and effort in roughly the following proportions:

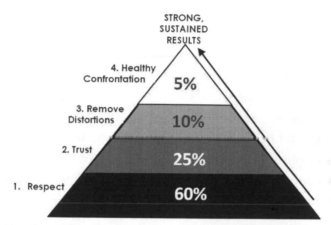

Relative time, effort, and energy required for each culture-building step

By now some readers may have discovered that there is a gift hidden in this process. You may have discovered that the process is relatively easy and can even be fun to do. We often associate pain with "people stuff." To the degree it is painful, it is painful precisely because of an approach that misunderstands human nature and the principles of culture, and it ignores this model. It is painful precisely because it is often about things like managing conflict or confronting someone without first having the foundations of respect and trust and without first having cleared away distortions. Of course an approach like that would be painful!

But imagine tackling any one of these four steps *after* first having established the step(s) that come before it. Sure it will take some skill and practice, but it won't be "painful." And in many cases, people and organizations that follow the model actually describe these steps as "fun."

* * * * * * *

Nothing is more certain than this: If an organization – *any* organization – does these four culture-building steps well, it will have a healthy, productive culture, and it will produce remarkable results. It doesn't matter if the organization sells shoes or computer services, whether it is full of gymnasts or is a blue collar place, whether it is a nonprofit or a bank or a lumber mill. It will deliver results that the leader can barely imagine.

The process all starts with listening and respect. And because that is the key, foundational part of the process, because that is the part that demands the vast majority of time and effort when building culture, it will receive its own short chapter. I will not go into detail about listening skills. I will not try to teach you all the proven techniques. I will not provide a comprehensive study of listening and how good listening creates an overall atmosphere of respect. But I will get you started. Once you get started on the deliberate effort to listen powerfully, you will begin to see small changes – and you will have begun the journey of intentionally creating a culture where people can perform at their very best. You will have begun something profound.

There are many resources that can help you with each step in the culture building process. I list our contact information on page 175. If you're serious about building a great culture, I encourage you to reach out to us. Others can help too. Just remember that many of the most helpful techniques are not innate; they are learned skills. Go get them.

Are you ready? Let's get started. Let's take a closer look at the most basic part of the culture building process: listening and respect.

CHAPTER 34

THE FOUNDATION: RESPECT (LISTENING)

If you decide to intentionally build culture, then understand this, absorb this, get this deep into your bones: *People want to be understood.*

Sure, they want to be agreed with. Sure, they want to be in charge and see things done their way. Sure, they want to be appreciated and thanked and recognized for having done something worthwhile. But all these are nothing when compared to people's desire to be understood. It is stronger than the desire to be praised, stronger than the desire to be treated fairly, and even stronger than the desire to act in their own self-interest. Perhaps only the instinctive desires for food and shelter can be said to be stronger that the desire to be understood.[5]

> "Perhaps one did not want to be loved so much as to be understood."
>
> *George Orwell*

People are not crazy; they are not irrational; they do not wake up wondering what they can do that day to be a thorn in the sides of others. But when they are frustrated from not being understood, they can appear so irrational and dysfunctional as to bewilder us. They can be self destructive. They can be combative. They can disrupt the flow of work, destroy relationships, anger customers, and behave in stunningly bad ways. They will sometimes even suffer incarceration,

---

[5] Maslow's Hierarchy of Needs lists physiological needs as our most basic, followed by our need for safety and then love and belonging. Then, as people move into the realm of factors that involves something akin to a work environment (i.e. beyond shelter, food, family and intimate relationships), esteem (which is entwined with being understood and respected) is our most fundamental need.

loss of employment, and destruction of families in the utter frustration that arises from their not being understood.

It may not be universally true that when people do feel understood, they all instantly become agreeable and compliant. But when faced with these seemingly irrational behaviors, listening is your best and often your only chance for success. When people feel understood, they feel valued. When people feel understood, they feel respected. And when people feel valued and respected, they suddenly have the ability to see themselves (and their behaviors) more objectively, and *they gain access to changing themselves in ways not previously possible.*

> "If I can listen to what they tell me;
> if I can understand how it seems to them;
> if I can see its personal meaning for them;
> if I can sense the emotional flavor which it has for them;
> then I will be releasing
> potent forces of change *in them*."
>
> *American Psychologist Carl Rogers*
> *Founder of Humanistic Psychology*
> [emphasis mine]

One particular story illustrates the critical importance of listening, understanding and respect, and it teaches us a key lesson as well. This story happened at CGA and was later used in training the staff, athletes, and families at CGA. I must warn you that it is almost too simplistic. It almost seems "magical," because it demonstrates how a few simple steps can almost instantly resolve a difficult situation. In that way, it can be hard to believe. Yet this story is true. Such is the power of listening and respect.

A group of CGA gymnasts, being active in local community causes, decided to raise money for a lifesaving piece of equipment for the Fairfield, Ohio, Fire Department. They needed to raise twenty thousand dollars, and planned to do that by placing donation jars at cash registers in the community and by sending fliers home with the

162

district's nine thousand school kids. The campaign would culminate with a gymnastics exhibition at the high school gym. There, in front of the whole community, they would present the new equipment to the fire department.

One day during the fundraising campaign, the gym's secretary came into Lynne's office and said, "Lynne, there's a lady who called in on the phone, and she's really mad. She's practically coming unglued. I have been on the phone with her for 10 minutes and now she is furious... you'd better take the call."

Lynne picked up the phone and punched the button that connected her to the caller. She barely got a "hello" out before the lady exploded in anger.

The caller yelled into the phone. "What are you doing down there?! How dare you?! I don't have money for this, you insensitive jerks! I've never seen a more

> People aren't irrational. But the frustration of not being understood can eventually drive them to behave irrationally.

incompetent bunch of do-gooder idiots – don't know your butts from a hole in the ground!" She went on like this, uninterrupted, for a full sixty seconds.

Lynne listened as best she could. Despite the defensiveness and resentment that automatically sprang up in Lynne's heart, she determined to simply listen and understand – no matter what.

When the caller finally took a breath Lynne said, "Wow, it seems you are really angry with us. And if I understand you correctly, you are mad because we sent a flier home from school with your son, asking you to donate money for a fire department that does not service the community where his school is located. And you feel we are pretty arrogant to ask you do contribute."

The caller, still agitated, but slightly less so, continued. "Yes, but that's not all. I had a fire in my home last summer and I lost everything."

Lynne said, "So, not only are we asking you for money to

support a fire department that doesn't service your part of Fairfield, but when you lost everything in a fire last year, they were not there for you."

By this time her voice was a little calmer when she replied. She said, "Yes, but that is not all. I am a Fire Fighter that services the other part of Fairfield, and I wish somebody cared enough about us to be raising money for a piece of life saving equipment for *us*."

Lynne said, "I am so sorry if my ignorance has caused you this kind of pain, because I didn't know there was another Fire Department that services Fairfield. If we raise enough money it would be an honor to buy a piece of life saving equipment for you as well."

The lady, finally feeling understood, softened. The conversation went on a bit longer, and Lynne stayed focused on simply trying to understand. They were getting ready to hang up when the lady surprised Lynne.

"Lynne, wait a minute," she said. "Please don't hang up. Could you please tell me who to make my check out to. I want to donate to your Fire Fund."

She sent in the largest donation that was received, $500 – from a woman who had lost everything the summer before, and who called with the single intent of venting her anger. Lynne's entire time on the phone with this lady lasted less than ten minutes.

> "The greatest compliment that was ever paid me was when one asked me what I thought, and attended to my answer."
> *Henry David Thoreau*

Do you remember how the parents strongly resisted the initial changes at CGA, how they threatened to leave and even practiced some sabotage? Because the leaders unfailingly practiced listening and respect, CGA never lost a single one of them.

Listening communicates respect. It helps people feel valued. That's powerful. And that's how you start building a great culture.

CHAPTER 35

SUMMARY OF LEARNING

1. *Culture drives results. It is more important than strategy.*
2. *People (all people) are created with remarkable talent and amazing potential – beyond what most of us can even imagine.*
3. *The core job and obligation of the leader is to draw that talent out and unleash it. The leader's job, indeed his/her duty, is to refine the gold that is already there.*
4. *The best way to do that is by managing culture. It is the single most significant thing any leader can do, and is the one thing that only they can do.*
5. *Culture is about the 1:1, everyday relational interactions in an organization. The core question is whether there is an assumption of human respect and dignity.*
6. *There is a proven, four-step model for building culture. It starts with respect (listening), and the steps must be pursued in sequence.*
7. *People want to be understood. It is a profound human desire. When they don't feel understood, they can quickly become irrational, uncooperative, non-compliant, and disruptive.*
8. *Listening is a learned skill, and it is as powerful a means of influencing others as speaking is.*
9. *When leaders get the culture right, human performance and organizational results soar.*

Our story began in 1983, when Lynne Ruhl took a phone call that would eventually come to change her world. She later received three promises that seemed to be so unlikely that they could have been called both ridiculous and outrageous. Indeed, they seemed impossible. Yet those promises have all come true.

But our story does not end there. It continues because those three promises were not just for Lynne and Mary Lee. They were for all of us. Those promises were for everyone who cares about organizations and performance – and people. Our story continues everywhere leaders are striving to improve bottom line results by creating cultures of profound dignity and respect. Our story continues today.

It continues with you.

APPENDIX

A Primer – Women's Gymnastics

Women compete and are scored by a panel of judges in four separate events. In competitive meets, gymnasts must perform "compulsories," in which each gymnast performs the exact same, standardized routine, providing direct comparisons; and "optionals," in which gymnasts develop and perform their own unique routines.

The events are as follows:

Vault

SPECIFICATIONS:
Vault horse/table: 14 inches wide, 4 feet high, 5 feet long
Springboard: made from laminated wood or fiberglass, with spring devices
Runway: 3 feet wide, 82 feet long

Depending on the type of vault selected by the gymnast, she must meet the requirements specified in the Code of Points, which also specifies the relative values of each skill performed. Among other things, judges look for a strong, accelerating run, how quickly and forcefully the gymnast gets her feet up over her head, how her hands are positioned, and the height and distance traveled in the second flight phase. Judges also look for the number and difficulty of saltos (flips) and twists; typically the more of each, the more the difficulty value of the vault.

Floor Exercise

SPECIFICATIONS:
Area: 40 feet x 40 feet square
Material: double-flex plywood floor layered with foam or rubber, covered with a soft elastic rubber or foam material, topped with a carpet-like material.

The routine must be 70 to 90 seconds, choreographed to music, and must cover the entire floor area. The gymnast must use acrobatic or gymnastics elements to create high points or peaks, including a series with two or more saltos, a series with great amplitude, and a series with considerable height and distance movement. Judges look for the gymnast to combine elements harmoniously and make versatile use of the floor space, with a dancer-like command of the music. They also look for impressive displays of flexibility and strength, and balance, all complimenting each other.

UNEVEN BARS

SPECIFICATIONS:
Length: 8 feet
Height: 5 feet lower bar, 8 feet upper bar
Width: 42 x 48 mm oval shaped bars
Material: wood laminated surface over fiberglass or steel cores; steel uprights and base

Routines must take the gymnast to both the upper and lower bars, incorporating many grip changes, releases and re-grasps, flight elements, changes of direction, saltos, and giant swings through the handstand position. Only four elements in a row may performed on the same bar, and movements should flow smoothly from one bar to the next. Judges particularly look for balance, precision, strength, big swings that incorporate hand changes and pirouettes, dismount elevation, complexity, and form in landing.

BALANCE BEAM

SPECIFICATIONS:
Width: 4 inches
Height: 4 feet
Length: 16 feet
Material: laminated wood beam topped with non-skid leather or synthetic material

Routines must last 70 to 90 seconds and cover the entire length of the beam. The gymnast must perform acrobatic moves to create high points or peaks, consisting of two or more elements performed in series, one immediately following the other. The gymnast must also perform elements that meet several specific criteria, such as an element close to the beam, a leap or jump with great amplitude, a turn on one leg of at least 360 degrees, etc. Judges look for balance and precision, a harmonious blend of movements and acrobatic elements, and an overall feeling that the routine is being performed on a floor 40 feet wide, rather than on a narrow 4 inch strip.

ACKNOWLEDGEMENTS

We are grateful to the many people who helped us bring this story and this book to life. Thanks especially to Mary Lee Tracy, Jaycie Phelps, Amanda Borden, Dr. Alison Arnold, and Becky Ruhl, all of whom were generous with their time and their perspective. We are also grateful to Kim Speed, Kim Quarry, Patty Borden, and Connie Hudson. Thanks to my wife, Sue, for her constant support. To Kim Kraus, Mary Preece, Mike Sipple, Gary Dittrich, Karin Maney, John Eckberg, Denis Beausejour, and Matthew Kelly for their critique, guidance and support. To all those who encouraged us along the way: Chuck Proudfit, Rob Stease, Terry Grear, Danise DiStasi, Ron Touby, Steve Simpson, Preston Bowles, Bob Pautke, Dave and Pam Ping, and all the others.

Most of all we are thankful to a Loving God who gives each of us talents and assigns purpose to our lives. To a God who reached into this true story and in so doing, gave it meaning for everyone who leads others.

ABOUT
THE AUTHORS

Gerry Preece is a consultant, writer and speaker with a unique background. After graduating from West Point and serving as an Army officer, he then spent twenty-two years at Procter & Gamble, culminating in his role as Global Director of Media and Marketing Sourcing. He then served as Executive Director for a national nonprofit organization before becoming a consultant. He is frequently invited to speak on a number of topics, including organizational culture and health, employee engagement, negotiations skills, the sourcing of marketing services, listening and trust building skills, and how organizational effectiveness hits the bottom line. Gerry has presented to wide range of audiences, from small groups to auditoriums of over a thousand. His audiences have included businesses, trade associations, civic groups, church groups, and academia. He has recently written a memoir, *Stories from the Farm on the Hill*, and is now working on his next book, which he hopes to have ready late in 2012. Gerry also continues to work with Lynne at Perfect 10 Corporate Cultures.

Lynne Ruhl is founder and CEO of Perfect 10 Corporate Cultures and she is a highly sought-after member of the National Speakers Association. She began her career as part of the Radio and Gift Shop Management Team for the Cincinnati Reds. Lynne stepped back from her career when she became a new mom, at least until she got that phone call in 1983, which brought her to Cincinnati Gymnastics Academy. She spent seventeen years as CGA's Culture Manager and lived the transformation experience that has been the focus of this book. In 2001, Lynne formed Perfect 10 Corporate Cultures as a way to spread the lessons of culture transformation. Lynne speaks to all kinds of groups on a number of culture-related topics, including celebrating the power of "you," managing in the new era, how "risk" is not a four letter word, how changing your beliefs can change your life, the remarkable power of listening, and many other topics regarding the importance and development of organizational culture.

ADDITIONAL RESOURCES

Visit this book's website for additional features,
including a powerful, six minute video summary of this story:
www.threeimpossiblepromises.com

    Today, Lynne Ruhl is the CEO of Perfect 10 Corporate Cultures™, a Cincinnati-based consultancy. Perfect 10 helps clients achieve better bottom line results by creating cultures where employees want to work and customers want to do business. We do this when clients are in urgent situations, at times in turnaround mode or working through significant challenges. We also do this with healthy, thriving businesses that are progressive-minded and seek ways to do even better. We evaluate cultures and we access information that is often inaccessible to an organization's leaders; we provide key insights and skill development; and we guide leaders and organizations through the various phases of intentionally building great cultures. For those organizations that earn it, Perfect 10 provides official culture certification. Perfect 10 Corporate Cultures calls out the greatness that already exists in every organization.

For more information, and to learn what you can do to help create a Perfect 10 Culture in your workplace, contact:

Perfect 10 Corporate Cultures™
P.O. Box 387, Loveland, OH 45140
www.perfect10cc.com
513-874-4220

lynne@perfect10cc.com
gerry@perfect10cc.com

www.perfect10cc.com

10003840R00117

Made in the USA
San Bernardino, CA
06 April 2014